Real Solutions
for Busy Moms

Real Solutions for Busy Moms

Your Guide to Success and Sanity

Kathy Ireland

with James Lund

HOWARD BOOKS

A DIVISION OF SIMON & SCHUSTER

New York London Toronto Sydney

Our purpose at Howard Books is to:
• *Increase faith* in the hearts of growing Christians
• *Inspire holiness* in the lives of believers
• *Instill hope* in the hearts of struggling people everywhere
Because He's coming again!

Published by Howard Books, a division of Simon & Schuster, Inc.
1230 Avenue of the Americas, New York, NY 10020
www.howardpublishing.com

Real Solutions for Busy Moms © 2009 by Kathy Ireland Worldwide

Library of Congress Cataloging-in-Publication Data

Ireland, Kathy.
Real solutions for busy moms: your guide to success and sanity / Kathy Ireland with James Lund.
p. cm.
Includes bibliographical references.
1. Mothers—Life skills guides. 2. Motherhood—Religious aspects—Christianity. I. Lund, James L. II. Title.
HQ759.I73 2009
248.8'431—dc22
2008024599

ISBN-13: 978-1-4165-6318-1
ISBN-10:   1-4165-6318-0

10 9 8 7 6 5 4 3 2 1

Manufactured in the United States of America

For information regarding special discounts for bulk purchases, please contact: Simon & Schuster Special Sales at 1-800-456-6798 or business@simonandschuster.com.

Edited by Between the Lines
Cover design by Stephanie D. Walker
Interior design by Jaime Putorti
Cover photo by Jonathan Exley © Kathy Ireland Worldwide

*This book is dedicated to the love of my life, whom
I love more with each passing year,
my amazing husband, Greg,
and the lights of our lives, our precious children,
Erik, Lily, and Chloe,
who bring us an overflowing wealth of joy.*

contents

acknowledgments

The Anchor to my soul, firm and secure . . . my Rock, my Light, my Lord and Savior and best friend, Jesus Christ . . . with Him all things are possible.

Mom and Dad . . . for your great, unlimited, unconditional love . . . always being there . . . your powerful prayers . . . for leading me to the Lord and teaching by example that all things, including faith, require work.

Barbara . . . so much more than a mother-in-law . . . Phil . . . forever in our hearts.

Aunt Dorothy . . . a pillar of strength.

My beautiful sisters, Mary and Cynthia . . . childhood adventures together, today you and your loving families inspire and delight.

Erik, Jason, Jon, and Stephen . . . family.

Erik . . . your quiet strength, your tremendous generosity, your brilliant and clever mind, your trust, your sense of adventure, your wisdom.

Jason . . . my mentor and so much more . . . for helping me find my voice . . . and an audience to listen! . . . for multiplying your gifts to bless others in powerful ways . . . your enormous heart, your clear, focused, and brilliant vision, your listening ears and open arms.

Jon . . . my bro, your fierce and secure protection, your

jovial and loving heart, your amazing eye and extraordinary talent . . . genius.

Stephen . . . your inspiring strength, your deep thoughtfulness, your loyalty, integrity, and brilliant and passionate genius that shatters limits.

Steve, Dee, Georgia, Miles, Konrad, Rocco, Ruben, Chris, Tony, Claude, Andre, Nicholas, Mitch, Joel, Zulma, Bart, Monica, Charlie, Maria, Felipa, Nittaya, and Millie . . . the best team in the world. Thank you to you, your spouses, your loved ones, and especially your children.

Brittany . . . beautiful and strong.

Camille, Baret, Jenny, Kim, Dawn, Michelene, Sue, Cheri, Wanda, Missi, Jule, Jeannine, and your beautiful families . . . for your prayers, friendship, love, and always giving more than you get.

Bessie . . . my hero . . . thank you for leading, teaching, and saving lives . . . you're a great inspiration! . . . love to you and your beautiful family.

Wyatt, Jacob, Joseph, Daniel, Sophia, Elijah, Junior . . . Sal, Mark, Grant, Dyan, Dana, and Paul . . . you mean more to me than words can express . . . you are treasures.

Our Niemann family leaders: Fritz, Linda, Camilla, Bill, Greg, Leila, Joe, Melinda, Tom, Jeri, Mary, Ron, Matt, Betty, Jim, and Sue . . . you and your families are amazing!

To our entire family tree with branches in Canada, England, Norway, and of course the USA.

Our Hawaii Ohana . . . Justin, Marisol, your beautiful sons and family . . . Kainoa, Bobbi Lee, and your families.

Peter Mainstain, Donna Melby, Miriam Wizman, and Tom Law and their companies . . . for support, protection, and love.

John and Marilyn Moretz . . . from the very beginning and forever . . . my love for you is too often unexpressed. That love is powerful and written on my heart.

Gavin Perdue and the team at Comerica Bank . . . for having faith in us when others did not.

Marilyn McCoo and Billy Davis, Jr. . . . for your gifts of love, friendship, and fellowship.

The Schuller family . . . for always giving warm welcomes and offering your hearts in friendship.

Anita and Roxy Pointer . . . brave, beautiful, and always so excited!

Tim Mendelson . . . with love and much appreciation.

The Estrada family . . . Erik and Nanette, great parents and great friends. Thank you for always giving so much to others . . . especially to us.

The Haskell family . . . Sam, Mary, Sam, and Mary Lane . . . your love, kindness, and leadership are off the charts. God bless you.

Joan van Ark and Jack Marshall for kindness and constant friendship.

Sim and Dr. Debra Farar . . . your friendship demonstrates the power of love, kindness, and brilliance. Thank you for loving and never judging.

To the Sedghi family . . . each of you is a precious jewel.

Effy and Leah Raps for true friendship and wisdom . . . in turbulence and beyond.

Kathy, Tony, and your glorious children for giving love and becoming family.

Harold and Dotty . . . you're an inspiration to us all! Marion, thank you for loving my guys.

Our brand partners, manufacturers, and retailers . . . for investing and believing every day.

Elise and the team at AEFK . . . for loving and changing lives.

Jonathan Exley, Kendra Richards, and José Manuel Morales . . . your creative gifts and love are extraordinary!

John and Chrys Howard and the team at Howard Books . . . our visit at the United Nations was the beginning of this book. Thank you for allowing moms everywhere to experience these solutions. May the love of our Lord surround you always.

James Lund . . . Jim, thank you for endless hours of extraordinary support . . . your great gifts as a writer and a man of faith brought this book to life. You made it possible for this book to be a conversation with busy moms rather than an "academic" effort.

The Tarte and Fisher families . . . for lasting friendship and indescribable adventures.

The Kuchmas family . . . for caring, for inspiring, for your friendship.

The Dellar family . . . for being examples and being with us.

The Providence Hall board, Randy, Greg, Cliff, Andrew, Stretch, Elise, Kelly, David, Joy, Jay, Paulette, Laura, Brian . . . commitment, passion, wisdom, and perseverance.

The Davies, the Dusebouts, and the ELMO board . . . leading with character and wisdom.

Pastor Britt, Pastor G, and your families . . . your tremendous love of our Lord, your faithfulness, commitment, and desire to serve Him.

Bible study ladies . . . your wisdom and encouragement.

The Merrick/Morgan home group and our entire church family . . . . wisdom and accountability with love for each other and Him.

Even with this list, there are so many people who made this journey and book possible who are not mentioned here. Please know my gratitude and love for you is strong. Scripture speaks of thanking God for each remembrance . . . whether named here or not, I give thanks for each and every one of you.

introduction

*Y*ou're a mom, and you feel like you're losing your grip. You feel overwhelmed. Underappreciated. Ready to resign. Do these descriptions fit your life? Please don't be defeated and desperate. Remember, you didn't always feel this way.

Somewhere along the line, the express train to the life of your dreams left the tracks. The wonderful picture you once had in mind for your future doesn't match the mess of your reality today. It's not even close. You're thinking, *How did I get here? Why is my life falling apart? What can I do to change this situation?*

You need solutions, and you need them now.

I share those feelings. As a wife and mother of three wonderful, precious, and very active children, and as a woman who feels overwhelmed more often than I like to admit, I understand! I'm right here with you. And I want to help—right now.

I am blessed with the power of knowing my priorities. They are faith, family, and the opportunity to pursue a fascinating career. My work includes designing, motivational speaking, writing, and serving as CEO of a home-products, lifestyle-design, and fashion company, Kathy Ireland Worldwide (KIWW). It's been a long, challenging, and interesting journey. Yet of all the jobs I have the privilege of pursuing, none is more difficult, demanding, rewarding, fulfilling, or empowering than the blessing of being Mom. Motherhood is the most important career in the world. If you are a mom, I believe you are a hero who deserves all the support the world can give you.

I communicate with moms every day: online, at the grocery store, at church, at speaking engagements, and on our company Web site. I understand and am grateful that you aren't coming to me for a beauty tip or an autograph or advice on how to dress. You tell me you're struggling with balancing the responsibilities of marriage, raising children, managing a household or career or both, and finding time to take care of yourself. You have financial concerns. You want more empathy or encouragement. You want personal growth. You want positive changes in your life. You need real solutions to the new problems you face every day, sometimes every minute.

At KIWW we are responsible for the design and marketing of more than fifteen thousand products sold in more than twenty-eight countries. Every one of those products must serve the family—especially mothers, who need solutions that work. You are my boss, and I'm grateful that you keep me and every member of our team on our toes. Our mission statement is

*" . . . finding solutions for families,
especially busy moms. "*[TM]

Those seven words influence every decision we make. We are committed to finding solutions for your life.

That's the reason for this book. Its purpose is to give you the tools and solutions you need to silence your inner critic, and the outer ones too, when you have them. Each chapter will help you win in life and realize the dreams that right now are alive only in your mind. Each chapter explores an area of life that speaks to one of the core issues that moms discuss daily: managing money; establishing a happy home environment; developing a healthy lifestyle; keeping children safe; finding and living your passion; making faith a priority; and balancing all of that with your personal needs as a mother. Each chapter includes a discussion section, a series of questions from busy moms with answers to give you the solutions you need. There's a checklist for helping you stay on track. And you'll find advice from experts to help you make your life and the lives of your family members happier, safer, healthier, wealthier, and more manageable.

This book will help you remove the obstacles that are blocking you from your dreams and your destiny. As we explore each chapter together, we'll tackle questions like these:

- Are you living the life of your dreams?

- Do you feel stuck and don't know how to get unstuck?

- Are you struggling with finances, and are you ready to see change in a powerful way?

- Do you want to live in a happy home?

- Are you doing everything possible to ensure that you and your family are healthy?

- Is your home safe?

- In addition to caring for your family, are you taking care of you?

- Are you pleased with the role of faith in your life?

With all the knowledge in these pages, I still work on these answers every day. Life and motherhood are challenging and sometimes scary. As moms, our responsibility to our families, particularly our children, is to feel our fear, walk through it, and do our best. From one mom to another, please know that your best is pretty amazing. You can make the changes you want—starting today—and begin enjoying the life you were meant to live. My prayer is that this book will be your first step.

It is a privilege to partner with you on this journey. May God bless you as we move forward together.

Love,
kathy

If you would like to contact kathy, please visit
www.kathyireland.com.

chapter one

Money Matters

I worry every day about our finances.

We never seem to have enough to pay our bills

and buy groceries, let alone get ahead.

What can we do?

*I*t can all be a deception.

You don't need me to tell you that millions of American families today are facing a financial crisis. Borrowing and over-spending have reached epidemic levels. According to recent figures, consumer debt in the United States is nearly $2.5 trillion. America's typical family credit card balance is 5 percent of their annual income; the median balance is $2,200.[1] This wave of overconsumption is leading to alarming trends: increased stress, health problems, marital strife (financial problems, marriage experts say, are the leading cause of divorce), and bankruptcies—and we're passing the same lessons and problems on to our children. It isn't happening to just one economic group either; it's the same whether you're earning $30,000 a year or $300,000. At every income level, our addiction to "more" is destroying the family as we know it.

When you stop to really look at family finances in this country, the picture is frightening. Many moms and dads have watched their savings and checkbook balances drop nearly to zero—or below zero—and are shaking their heads and asking themselves, How did we get here? The answer, I believe, is that we're often chasing an illusion of prosperity—or trying to maintain one. Either way, it's a dangerous fantasy.

You may know that earlier in my career, I worked as a model. That's when I first realized how much of what we see every day is an illusion. The final product that the public sees in a magazine is a glossy image of a model on a beach in some exotic location. I know, however, that someone has digitally retouched every wrinkle and drop of perspiration, enhanced the blues in the sky and the oranges of the sun's rays, and even bleached the grains of sand. When I modeled, I sometimes barely recognized the picture that came out in the magazine of a photo shoot I was in! It might have been a beautiful scene, but it didn't match the reality I remembered.

We're bombarded daily with these illusions. On television advertisements we see perfect, smiling families from perfect homes driving perfect cars on perfect vacations. We watch famous men and women wearing dazzling evening gowns and expensive jewelry accept awards on stage for their achievements. Closer to home, we notice that our neighbors down the street have parked a new boat or RV in their driveway. And we think, *Everyone else has those things. I want them too.* What we forget is that the people on TV are actors being paid to promote a product, the dresses and jewelry may be rentals, and your neighbors may have taken on debilitating debt to finance their latest purchase. The image is a deception.

Are you chasing any illusions? If you're dealing with credit card debt, if you find yourself saying yes to purchases for nonessentials even when your head is telling you no, or if your lifestyle leads people to think you have more money than you really do, my guess is that you're pursuing something you'll never find by spending money. It's like those greyhounds at the dog races that chase a mechanical rabbit along a rail around the track—no matter how fast those dogs run, they'll never catch that little guy.

In this chapter we'll talk about how to get you into a different race—one you can win. Let's start with the three primary reasons why people buy into the illusion of prosperity.

Reason 1: False Impressions

The first reason people put on a front of prosperity is that they're trying to impress others. In my generation, we call it "keeping up with the Joneses." It means buying things you don't really need or want to make an impact on someone you may not even know or like. It can apply to almost anything—your clothes, your car, your home, your furniture, your yard, what and where you choose to eat. The idea is to show off wealth you don't really have so that someone somewhere will think better of you. You might even be trying to make yourself think better of you.

The funny thing is that most people of great financial wealth don't feel the need to show it. I have the privilege of occasionally spending time with Warren Buffett, who owns Shaw Industries, our magnificent flooring partner that gave us our start in the home industry. I was introduced to Mr. Buffett by my friend Irv Blumkin, president of Nebraska Furniture Mart, which also is one of Mr. Buffett's Berkshire Hathaway companies. I met Mr. Blumkin at our first furniture market ten years ago.

The Blumkin family is legendary. Mr. Blumkin's grand-mother Rose was a hero of mine. I still enjoy reading about this remarkable woman who made her way from Russia to the United States when she was in her twenties. She began her new life with sixty-six dollars and no knowledge of English, yet was able to start a small furniture store in the basement of her husband's pawn shop. Her motto was, "Sell cheap and tell the truth." That modest operation grew into what today is a retail giant. Rose died a multimillionaire at the age of 104.

Mr. Buffett was impressed with Rose Blumkin, too. One of the many things I admire about him is that even though he is one of the wealthiest people in the world and can afford every lavish excess, he enjoys a simple lifestyle. He's lived in the same house in Omaha, Nebraska, for nearly fifty years, and his big extravagances each day are drinking Cherry Coke and eating a Dairy Queen ice-cream dessert.

Have you thought about the difference between people who choose high living over high net worth? The first group may earn tremendous salaries but spend their money as fast or faster than it comes in. Despite their income, they're always broke. The second group may earn far less, but because they are frugal with their earnings, they're able to save and achieve financial security. Most of today's millionaires don't shop at Saks Fifth Avenue or Neiman Marcus. They prefer more af-fordable chains and independent retailers. That's the attitude that made them millionaires.

Are you spending more than you earn in an effort to im-press people around you? If you are, it's a bit like buying a Hal-loween costume you can't afford (one that just as easily could have been made at home), then going out trick-or-treating.

And when the night is over, you don't have any treats, and the trick is that you've lost all your money, too.

Reason 2: Possession Obsession

The second reason people may chase prosperity illusions is that they have adopted a sense of entitlement. They've decided that since everyone else is enjoying the high life, they should, too. They feel that they deserve the best, whether they can afford it or not. You could say they're afflicted by "possession obsession." The words *save* and *sacrifice* are not part of their vocabulary. It is a shortsighted approach to managing your money and your life.

I'm reminded of a woman I knew who, at the pinnacle of her career, chose only the finest luxuries, wore the most extravagant designer clothing, and traveled in the largest limousines. In three short years her career ended. Her annual income dropped from $2 million a year to nothing. This woman became ill and wound up in a hospital. Unfortunately, she had failed to plan for the future; she had no savings whatsoever. She also had no health insurance and had to rely on state aid. When she died, she was literally homeless. It is a sad and common story, but it doesn't need to be your story.

I encourage you to take an honest look at your attitude toward possessions and money. If you're making financial decisions based on the idea that you deserve something, you also may be taking your family on the road to possession obsession. I urge you to turn around before you drive off a cliff. If you ruthlessly evaluate each potential purchase and make your decision based on need rather than a feeling of entitlement, you'll be heading in the right direction.

Reason 3: Trying to Fill a Void

The third reason so many people chase or try to maintain an illusion of prosperity is that we're trying to fill a void in our life. Something in our heart and soul is missing. Maybe we have a low opinion of ourselves and are trying to raise our self-image through purchases. We may be ashamed of our financial status and spend money on items we can't afford in hopes of temporarily relieving that shame. Perhaps we're lonely or brokenhearted. And we all know people who attempt to replace the priceless gift of time with material things. In a divorced family, it may happen to a father who is no longer in the home or a mother who feels guilty about the absence of that father.

I know a couple with two young boys. The father is a confirmed workaholic and frequently buys gifts for his sons in an attempt to make up for missing special events. In one case he had the family reschedule a birthday celebration so he could pursue a work opportunity, even though his family already has enough money to enjoy a luxurious life.

Money and the things it can buy are never the answer to a deep emotional hurt or need. Jesus said, "Be on your guard against all kinds of greed; a man's life does not consist in the abundance of his possessions" (Luke 12:15). Jesus also said: "No servant can serve two masters. . . . You cannot serve both God and Money" (Luke 16:13). When we chase after money and believe it will solve all our problems, we're really allowing money to be our master. We're putting our faith in something that ultimately will let us down. We must make money our servant, not the other way around.

I believe these three things—false impressions, possession obsession, and trying to fill a void—are the most common reasons people chase after prosperity illusions, but they certainly aren't the only causes of family struggles with finances. Some people are afraid of money. I used to be. We won't invest because we fear losing our savings, and we end up missing opportunities. Some of us are so discouraged with our financial situation that we've given up on anything ever changing and don't even try. Others just seem addicted to compulsive spending. In every case, we and the people we love suffer the consequences. It doesn't have to be this way. Please know that I understand this, because I've been there.

The Right Attitude

When it comes to financial issues, most people believe that more money will solve their problems. They think, *If I can just land that new, higher-paying job* . . . or *If Mom will just lend me some money* . . . or *If only that lottery ticket will come through this time, then we'll be back on track.* If your tendency is to spend every dollar that comes in, for whatever reason, more money will never solve anything. You'll always be scrambling to get by, always struggling with debt, and always living from one paycheck to the next. Perhaps worse, you'll be teaching your children to do the same.

As a young girl I always understood the value of a dollar

and the satisfaction of having my own money. For the three and a half years I had a paper route, I put away twenty dollars each month in a savings account. Those savings allowed me to take a month off before starting a new job and eventually made it possible for me to purchase my first car.

A few years later, as I gained some success in my modeling career and started earning a steady income, I began to pay less attention to saving. I bought a fancy condo at the beach, which added a high mortgage payment to my expenses. Looking into the rearview mirror of my life, I could have made a better investment buying a house or rental property that was inland. That would have given me income possibilities in an emergency. But no . . . I loved the beach, and the beach I got. A savvy investor might have been concerned, but I wasn't worried. That lack of discipline caught up with me one day when I blew out my knee while skiing. Suddenly I was in a cast and unemployable in my career field. My savings were too meager to cover my luxury life at the beach. No bank was interested in loaning more money to an overage model (at twenty-five, I was pushing the envelope) on crutches. Finally a finance company agreed to give me a loan—at a steep interest rate.

That experience was a powerful lesson for me. It taught me the importance of living beneath my means rather than at or just above what I could afford. I got back to the philosophy that had worked so well when I had that paper route: I made sure to set aside a specific portion of my income every month. Soon I had an emergency fund built up again, one that eased my concerns about the future. That paid off several years later, when I faced another financial challenge. At the time our company did most of its business with one major retailer, which filed for bankruptcy and threw our finances into a tailspin. I had to use my home and other personal assets to keep our company and our thirty-seven employees afloat. I wouldn't have had this option if my own finances hadn't been in order.

In the rest of this chapter, I'd like to offer you a number of proven strategies that will help you get a handle on your family's financial situation. Every one of them is effective in its own way. Bringing in more money and learning how to manage it is not the only solution. The key to achieving financial success for you and your family can be found only in maintaining a healthy relationship with money. Remember, you are the mistress and your money is your servant. When we're willing to stop chasing illusions, break any emotional ties we have to spending, and make money work for us, then, moms, we're on our way.

Real Solutions

PROBLEM: Our lives are so crazy that I only balance my checkbook when the bank statement comes in the mail. Is that so bad?

SOLUTION: Establish a financial plan.

It's best to balance your checkbook as you write each check. You asked whether waiting for your bank statement is so bad. It's not so much a question of it being "bad." In a way, it's worse than bad—it's dangerous! You can find yourself in big trouble. You could accidentally bounce checks. This wreaks havoc with your budget, damages your credit rating, and in extreme cases can even send you to jail. When I was ten years old, in one of my early business ventures, someone wrote me a bad two-dollar check, and I bartered freshly baked cookies for the services of a kind private detective. He helped me collect my money. The people who wrote the check were kind—and embarrassed. Clearly, they weren't on top of their finances.

It is astonishing that so many people don't know exactly what they're spending, how much money they have, and what their financial goals are for the future. To handle your finances well, it is vital that you keep a budget and establish a financial plan. If you're married and your spouse is the one handling your money, it's equally important for you to know where you stand, whether you're looking at debt or assets. That way, whatever happens, you're prepared.

If you've never kept a budget, start now. You can choose from a wealth of available information that explains how to begin and gives you sample budgets. On your own, you can start writing down your expenditures and dividing them into categories: savings, housing, child care, insurance, transportation, entertainment, clothing, etc. You may be surprised to see what you're spending in certain areas compared with others. Is your spending supporting or sabotaging your priorities and goals? What we do has a bigger impact on our lives than what we say. Once you get a picture of how much you're spending on one thing versus how much you spend on something else, you realize that you're in charge. Make your plan and stick to the plan!

Just as important as establishing a budget is knowing what you want your financial picture to look like in the future. I recently spoke at a conference on entrepreneurialism. I got the attention of the audience by saying, "Money, money, money, everybody says they want more money. Who here would like to have more money? You can have it right now!" Immediately most of the hands in the room went right up. I walked over to a man in the front row and handed him a crisp bill but in a small denomination. "Is that what you had in mind?" I asked. He looked disappointed, shook his head, and politely said "No."

"You said you wanted more money," I continued, "and now you have more money." The problem for this man, as for many of us, is that he wasn't specific about what he wanted. He just wanted "more."

I had a very different experience when I spoke in 2007 at the United Nations to a group of devoted young people invited by the United Nations' Youth Assembly. The topic of this annual conference was social entrepreneurship, and these people, from teenagers to adults in their twenties, were acutely aware of the power and potential of each dollar. Many of these young leaders were from developing countries. They were using their passion and money to purchase desperately needed clean wells and drinking water; develop and support programs that encourage female empowerment; invest in non-profit organizations that fight HIV/AIDS; and work on-site to battle malaria and hunger and clean up the environment. Their agenda? Changing the world. They had goals and plans for how to realize them. I was so impressed with these young people. I pray for their continued success. They know that a dream without a specific plan and timetable is just a hallucination. They know that a well-conceived financial blueprint can change lives forever.

To help you set and achieve your financial goals, I encourage you, when you can afford it, to consider getting help from legitimate resource professionals. When your car breaks down, don't you go to a mechanic? No blame, no shame. Fixing money matters is more critical than auto repair, yet sometimes we're reluctant to get the help we need. Why? We may be ashamed of our financial ignorance and economic status. If that's your situation, don't let it stop you. We've all been there. Shame over money is a destroyer. The cost of a little embarrassment will be far less than what you'll gain by following a wise financial course.

When shopping for a financial adviser, carefully check references, and never sign any documents you don't fully understand. If you can't afford a certified public accountant, consult a nonprofit credit counseling service. Many Christian organizations provide these services at no cost. And if you can't afford to buy this book, please contact me through your local library, through your church, or at www.kathyireland.com, and we'll make one available to your library or church.

My financial planner, who has become my friend, is Miriam Wizman. I appreciate Miriam's advice and cherish our friendship. Yet I always evaluate her advice before acting on it. No matter who advises you, you must make your own decisions. It's like having a driving instructor. You can learn a great deal from that person, but once you put the key in the ignition and start the engine, you are responsible. Even if you've obtained the services of an adviser you're comfortable with, your financial direction must be under your control.

PROBLEM: I should do a better job of saving. I just can't face it—it's too hard.

SOLUTION: Learn to sacrifice.

Believe me, I know how overwhelmed moms and their families can be by the pressures of life. I understand that there are some things you're tempted to ignore, but sticking your head in the sand—what I call "ostriching"—won't work when it comes to your money. You've got to pull your head out and look at your finances. Face the fear. Make the changes. If you don't, eventually someone or something else will do it for you. That something could be foreclosure, bankruptcy, the inability to retire, or medical bills you cannot pay. That's a high price for a game of ostrich.

Ask yourself this hard question: is your life putting you in debt and killing your future? If so, it's imperative that you stop hiding and make some tough decisions. Deep down, we know when we're in trouble. Sometimes we just keep trying to ignore that inner voice of reality. Depending on your circumstances, becoming more conservative with your expenditures might be enough to get you back into the black. Maybe you just need to do little things like taking your lunch to work each day instead of eating out. Maybe, like someone in my life whom I love dearly, you need to give up your car and ride the bus to and from work so the money you would have spent on car payments can be put to better use. Over time, those types of small steps add up to big savings.

I love the story about a man who never earned a salary of more than forty thousand dollars a year and never had an employer contribute to his retirement fund, yet at age sixty-five retired with a $2.5 million portfolio. He did it by living a simple and frugal lifestyle. If you start today and invest less than ten dollars a day, in four decades with an 8 percent annual return, you'll be a millionaire.

Please stop thinking about money only in terms of today. You'll need more money in maturity. Saving for a university education for your children is important, but community college is a wonderful option, too. Encourage your kids to work to qualify for scholarships that will make access to the best schools possible and affordable. Why go into megadebt for your children's college before you know how to fund your own retirement? Most Americans have saved less than ten thousand dollars for their retirement. Should Social Security collapse, most of us will, too. You don't want to get yourself in a situation where you're on the streets in your sunset years and your kids need to bear your financial burdens.

If your financial problems are severe right now, it's time to let go of things you thought were important, to accomplish what's truly important. One example: if you live in an area with a high cost of living and are making high rent or high mortgage payments, consider relocating to a place where living expenses and real-estate values are lower. It's hard, and it's scary, sure—but you can do it. And what a long-term blessing it will be to escape from that ever-present burden of debt! Expect to make some sacrifices on the way to a better financial future, but be encouraged that once you commit to making those tough choices, your life will begin turning around before you know it.

PROBLEM: I can't keep up with my credit card payments—in fact, I'm falling further behind every month.

SOLUTION: Pick up the phone.

We've already discussed a few of the grim statistics about credit card debt. Let me share one more: according to the Federal Reserve, approximately 60 percent of credit card users in the United States do not pay off their balances in full each month.[2] That means that millions and millions of American families are carrying what I call "enemy debt"—debt to a lender for expenditures that likely have no lasting value, and debt that is increasing at an interest rate frequently between 18 and 23 percent, none of which is tax deductible. This is not a place you want to be.

So, you're one of those millions of American families?

Okay. Let's face it and begin figuring out what to do about it. I recommend the following five steps:

1. Pick up the phone and dial the number of your credit card company. Explain that you're having financial problems, and ask them to lower the interest rate. Too intimidated? Remember, the card companies don't want you to sink so low financially that they lose you as a customer. I was visiting a friend recently who told me she was paying 23 percent interest on her credit card debt. I said, "What are you doing?" I made her pick up the phone— I dialed the number of her credit card company for her—and told her to explain what she needed. She eventually reached a supervisor and revealed that she could no longer meet her payments at the current rate. After fifteen minutes on the phone, her interest rate had been lowered from 23 to 8 percent. Eight times out of ten, if you ask, that's what will happen.

2. If you own a home, take out a home equity line of credit and transfer your credit card debt there. You'll probably get a much lower interest rate, and it may be tax deductible. With today's credit crunch, it won't be easy. Go for it anyway.

3. Explore ways to bring in extra funds to pay off your debt. If you tap the entrepreneur within you, you'll uncover all kinds of possibilities. Maybe you can host a yard sale. Maybe you have items that would bring a nice return on eBay. If you're a stay-at-home mom, could you babysit some of your friends' children or take on a few neighborhood sewing projects? Consider borrowing from your retirement savings, and then pay yourself back rather than the credit card company.

Another option is to take on a second, part-time job. I don't believe anyone should work twenty-four hours a day, seven days a week, especially busy moms and their families. The costs to your marriage and your relationships with your children are too great. However, this may be a time when you need to temporarily increase your working hours to eliminate enemy debt. Whatever work you do, if it's one of your passions and among your God-given gifts, you'll find that it's almost no work at all. If you dream of someday having your own catering business, working in the food service industry can be interesting and a great step in that direction. If fashion design is your passion, working in a clothing store might bring you joy. If all this fails, you just might need to determine that housing and feeding your family is your passion. Your fulfillment can come from knowing that you're serving your loved ones.

My husband, Greg, a person I am amazed by and proud of, is an emergency-room physician. He also loves to fish. He decided a few years ago that fishing might be a way to bring in additional money for some of the nonprofit organizations we support. Greg acquired a commercial fishing license and turned a fun hobby into a profitable new venture.

Of course, if you have a regular job, one of the obvious ways to bring in more money is to ask your boss for a raise. Many people dismiss this idea because they're afraid. They don't know how to negotiate an increase in earning power. I'll give you a hint: never tell your employer that you need a raise because you're having money troubles. That's not your company's problem. Instead, state what you've been doing in your job, explain the value of your performance, compare what you're making now to what your position might merit in another company, and ask for a fair salary adjustment. If your request is rejected, ask what steps you can take to get the kind of increase you're seeking. Schedule a performance review to talk about the matter again. Politely put your employer on notice that you plan to do a wonderful job and expect to be paid appropriately. In business and in life, you frequently don't get what you deserve. You get what you negotiate.

4. Do everything you can to pay more than your credit card's minimum monthly payment. My dad is from England, and the English call minimum payments the "never-never plan" because you never pay anything off. The only way to gain ground is to increase those monthly payments or, even better, to make payments twice a month. And be sure you don't miss a payment—even one late check can increase your interest rate and lower your credit score, which determines your ability to get a mortgage or borrow for any purpose at the lowest available interest rate.

5. Convert to cash. If none of the above methods is sufficient, it's time to convert to a cash system and lock up your credit cards in a safe, remote place where they can only be used for emergencies (which, by the way, do not include treating your friend to lunch on her birthday). Better yet, cut those cards into little pieces so you won't even be tempted. It will be painful and cause you some inconvenience; but if you persevere, it's guaranteed to work. As motivational speaker Anthony Robbins says, "Determination is the wake-up call to the human will."

One other note: unless you have absolutely no alternative, don't even think about bankruptcy as a solution to your debt troubles. People today are much too comfortable with walking away from their commitments. It's as if everything is disposable. When you borrow money or go into debt, you are making an agreement to repay that debt. As Jesus said in the Bible, "Simply let your 'Yes' be 'Yes,' and your 'No,' 'No'" (Matthew 5:37). There are exceptions to this rule, of course— a devastating medical bill, a death in the family that drastically alters your financial circumstances, or a situation in which you are the victim of fraud. However, these events are rare. When you fail to honor your financial agreements, you damage more than your credit rating. Bankruptcy will destroy your reputation and your self-confidence. Most of the time, it is a poor solution.

If you're facing foreclosure on your home, negotiate with your lender the same way you would with your credit card company. Lenders don't want your house. They want money. Their notices scare you, and your silence scares them. Get on the phone or go to a local branch and speak with your lender. From credit cards to car loans, negotiate and renegotiate. It's sensible. It's survival.

PROBLEM: How can I even think about investing when we're barely getting by?

SOLUTION: Start where you are.

One of the most important elements of any financial plan is a strategy for building up savings and investments. From my conversations in person and by e-mail with mothers across the country, I'm reminded every day that moms already feel that they're pinching every penny to get by. When I said earlier in this chapter that I set aside a portion of my income every month, I could almost hear the response: "That's easy for you to say, Kathy, but every week we're down to the bone. We don't have anything to invest!"

Believe me, I understand how hard it is to invest. I've witnessed astounding levels of poverty. As a little girl growing up in California, I watched field workers labor hour after hour in the sun for nearly nothing. I was less than ten years old when I marched in picket lines and attended rallies with César Chávez to support my father's union efforts to help workers receive fair treatment, including sanitation facilities. It's tough to focus on long-term gains when you're not sure you'll have money for groceries on Saturday. Yet if you're patient and take the responsibility to plan for your family's future, you can significantly change your financial circumstances.

The key is simply to start where you are. One basic strategy is to take out a dime for every dollar of income. If a dime is too much, try for a nickel, or even a penny. Some months you may be able to do better than that and have a hundred dollars or a thousand dollars to place in savings. Other months, it may be closer to ten dollars. As long as it's something, you can begin building a nest egg that can be used for profitable investments.

When you're in a position to invest those savings in higher-interest areas, the word you want to remember is *diversify*. Remember the major retailer I mentioned that went into bankruptcy and completely disrupted our business finances? At that time we were too dependent on one partner. We hadn't yet learned—I hadn't learned—to diversify. You may want to consider real estate (always a great buy, and especially so in a depressed market, as we've experienced recently), the stock market, mutual funds, and municipal bonds. Be willing to look at "friendly debt," the opposite of the enemy debt I mentioned earlier. Friendly debt is incurred when you invest in something, often real estate, that is expected to increase in value over time. Yes, there is always an element of risk in investing, but when you spread out that risk, chances are excellent that you'll end up where you want to be—with your money working for you.

Once you do reach the point of having money to set aside each month for savings or investments, you'll also have other wonderful opportunities. If you're making a monthly mortgage payment, for example, consider increasing your payment or adding an extra payment each year—you'll be surprised at how much this will reduce your principal. Or make a bonus payment to your children's college education fund. And please don't think only of your own family. You can do an amazing amount of good for others and bring joy to your own heart when you put even a little money to work. Is there a nonprofit organization whose work you've always admired? A deserving family you want to help? Like the ripples from a pebble dropped into a pond, your generosity can spread in so many directions that you'll never fully realize how many people you've helped and encouraged. When you give, you lose your fear of money and turn it into joy.

I must add that because of my faith, tithing is very important to me. The Bible says a great deal about money and giving, including "Be sure to set aside a tenth of all that your fields produce each year" (Deuteronomy 14:22). I believe that everything, including my money, belongs to God. I encourage you to pray and read God's Word to see what He says on this topic. I believe God blesses people in different ways at different times in their lives. God is faithful to His promises. He has blessed us already. He sees all, including our obedience to Him.

PROBLEM: I'd like to give, but on my income I can't afford it. Even if I did give, it's a small amount. Would it make any difference?

SOLUTION: Give what you can—no gift is too small.

When I spoke to that audience of young people at the United Nations, we discussed eight Millennium Development Goals that ranged from halving extreme poverty to providing universal primary education and reducing the spread of devastating diseases. To accomplish these initiatives, many of us will be forced out of our comfort zones. That's okay. Our comfort is irrelevant. The three thousand people in Africa dying each day of malaria know nothing of comfort. It takes so little to make a difference. For just five dollars we can buy mosquito netting that will protect an entire family.

When my husband is fishing on his boat and lets out his traps, he has time to think. He came up with a concept he calls the Dollar Project. His inspiration was Jesus' parable of the talents, in which two servants make wise investments with their master's money and increase it. They are contrasted with a third servant, who hides the money entrusted to him in the ground and earns nothing (Matthew 25:14–30). Greg's idea was to teach kids to be entrepreneurial and to be of service by taking just one dollar and using it to make positive change in the world.

This is also a great project for adults. I was excited by the challenge—in fact, my brainstorming started keeping me up at night. I turned to that great time-saving research tool, the Internet. When I typed in the words "one dollar nonprofit developing countries" and initiated a search, I was amazed at the results. Eventually I chose a company called Tiny Stitches, located in a small Georgia town. One dollar buys a needle and thread and puts them in the hands of a gifted sewer, who then makes blankets and clothing for babies in need.

You *can* be generous without compromising your own financial stability—just don't allow yourself to be manipulated into giving more than you want. Learn to give and let go. Give freely; a gift with an expectation is a bribe. There are so many opportunities to help others. We just need to open our eyes and give with a cheerful heart.

PROBLEM: I admit it, I'm an impulse buyer. Sometimes my checkbook seems to have a mind of its own! Can you help me?

SOLUTION: Do your research before you shop.

Especially with the advent of the Internet, there really is no reason to make impulse purchases before doing your research on a product you want to buy. Read reviews. Talk to friends. Ask yourself, Do I want this product because of its quality or because of its brand? Do I need it at all? Can I buy it used? No one believes in the brand concept more than I do. Some brands promise, "Buy this product and you'll discover a level of luxury that will change your life." Our brand at Kathy Ireland Worldwide is built around affordability, practicality, and quality. A little research and thought into what you're buying and why will make you a much wiser consumer.

The same strategy applies to investing. Thanks to a 2002 law called the Sarbanes-Oxley Act, public corporations must be more transparent than ever about their financial state. When considering a business investment, learn everything you can about that company's history and financial practices and performance. Do the same for other investments you're weighing, whether they're real estate, the stock market, or a certificate of deposit. Your research won't guarantee success, but it will give you a much better idea of which companies and investments are most stable and most likely to perform well in the future. The knowledge you gain even from a loss can give you the insight you need to earn high returns on your money for years.

Even after research there likely will be times when we lose money. I've lost money in the past, and I expect I will again. The key is to win more often than we lose. Investments, partnerships, and purchases don't always succeed. In failure, be grateful for your PhD (paid in hard dollars) education and move on to the next opportunity.

PROBLEM: I think we might have insurance, but to be honest I'm not even sure how much or what kind. What do I do?

SOLUTION: Protect your family and your money.

As a parent it is extremely important that you provide for your family by obtaining adequate health insurance, life insurance, and retirement savings. Because of the rapidly rising cost of health care and insurance premiums, millions of Americans today are uninsured. I understand the problem. I also know that these people are leaving themselves and their families at great risk. When it comes to health insurance, I don't believe anyone can be overinsured. I urge you to do what you can to protect your family. Shop around and compare rates and coverage plans. Talk to friends who have done the same. Any coverage, even if it's through a state-coordinated program, is better than no coverage at all.

Do the same for life insurance and retirement plans. Investigate. Talk to your financial adviser if you have one. Look into term life insurance, which tends to be the most affordable choice. If you have a 401(k) plan at work that includes an employer matching contribution program, take advantage of it. If you don't have a 401(k) plan, consider opening an IRA. Know where these retirement monies are invested. Monitor them. Start where you can, and know that over time your initial investment will build on itself.

It's not enough, though, simply to put these insurance and retirement plans in place. You must be vigilant in continuing to compare rates and plans and in making sure you're being properly charged and credited. Did you know that if the government makes a mistake and shortchanges your social security fund, after four years it can't be corrected? Do you know your Fair Isaac Corporation (FICO) credit score, which determines your ability to borrow? It's your money, and it's your responsibility, so do everything you can to protect it.

PROBLEM: I'm a working mother, but I usually rely on my husband to keep our budget and make all the financial decisions. I'm just not that comfortable with money. Is that okay?

SOLUTION: Get on to your financial team.

The short answer is, no! All moms work, whether they get paid or not. Being a stay-at-home mom doesn't absolve us from ignorance about money. And being a mom with a job outside the home doesn't magically bestow us with financial savvy. Some of us moms have a tendency to avoid financial matters for many reasons. We feel we don't have enough experience handling money. We fear being more emotional than analytical. We're simply too busy. We believe that if our husband is the primary wage-earner, he should be the one to control the family's finances.

Some moms don't have that option. As thousands of single mothers already know, most moms are more than capable of making wise financial decisions and managing a budget.

I'm not saying you should try to push your partner out of the financial picture. Why not work as a team? I encourage you and your husband to sit down together when it's time to pay the bills and make financial decisions jointly. Talk through any issues that arise. Each of you will have valuable input, and it's a process that will lead to better financial choices and improved communication in your marriage.

PROBLEM: I'm a recently divorced mother of two. I'd like to build a long-term career to support my kids financially. As a woman in a career dominated by men, is it possible?

SOLUTION: Don't limit yourself.

When your daily responsibilities as mom include changing diapers or preparing family meals, it may be hard to imagine yourself managing a team of talented professionals or taking the lead in a new corporate venture. But I say, why not? You're already CEO of your home. You have skills and abilities you haven't even discovered yet. Don't buy into the myth that we can't succeed in high-level careers or achieve financial success. That's just sexist noise. I remember, when I started my brand, a man telling me that I couldn't have any real interest in business. He thought I just wanted to "make a few bucks and make a few babies." I don't know where that man is today. I wasn't surprised when his company went out of business. You *can* succeed. You *can* live your dreams. It's okay to make reaching those goals a priority. For me, they're just not *the* priority—I believe faith and family should always come first. And as we've discussed, making money simply to acquire more stuff isn't a healthy approach to life. Yet I see no reason to limit yourself in the areas of career and finances. Go for it!

I am fortunate to know two women who have enjoyed tremendous success as entrepreneurs and, who are pioneers in the field of brand building. Martha Stewart has drawn on her background in catering, home remodeling, cooking, and gardening to establish a wide-ranging business enterprise that has made her one of the most well-known names in America. When Martha went to prison, the media called our office constantly for comments. "Is Martha finished?" the headlines screamed. No way! Martha tuned out the noise, served her time, came out of the pokey, and spent $50 million buying out the Emeril brand. Martha is always ready for change. She is amazing. She moves forward.

Jaclyn Smith became well known as a popular and accomplished actress. When I was younger, I enjoyed watching her battle the bad guys and win on *Charlie's Angels* every week. Years later she launched her own brand of hugely successful women's apparel and, later, home furnishings. I was honored when our team at KIWW was invited to share our expertise and consult with Jaclyn when she followed us into the home market.

These are just two examples of leaders who rejected the idea that women can't flourish in business. Both of these pioneers are mentors to me who proved that you can change careers brilliantly and successfully in your middle years. Martha and Jaclyn didn't let age, family, or discrimination serve as a barrier, and if you look, you'll find many more examples of moms who are saying yes to opportunity.

I admit that when our one big retail partner went bankrupt, it was scary for me to leave the nest of security and go out on my own to build thousands of business relationships instead of one. Yet today our company is more successful than we ever imagined. With God's help and the support of our team and partners, I'm learning to fly—and so can you.

I'm mindful of a dear friend and mother I love who has had many careers: Academy Award–winning actress, fragrance designer, art and jewelry collector, jewelry designer, entrepreneur, and most important, world-changing philanthropist. Elizabeth Taylor was a sparkling sixty years old when she launched her White Diamonds perfume. Sixteen years later, she's still a leader in that industry, and celebrities flock to copy what she does every day. Many more such female leaders are out there, and you can be one of them.

PROBLEM: I'm realizing that I haven't taught my kids anything about how to handle money. What should I do first?

SOLUTION: Start with financial fundamentals.

If your family is like most American families, you probably don't talk much about money in front of your children, especially if you're struggling. You may feel ashamed of your situation and not want your kids to worry about the future or whether you can afford to send them on next week's band trip. Part of that practice may come from the fact that our parents and grandparents didn't speak to us about money. In previous generations, the subject of family finances was often closed to children.

Let's not do that to our kids. It's never too early (or too late) to educate children about the fundamentals of handling money. From the beginning, give your kids an understanding of where you are financially, what you have, and what you can and cannot afford to do. Give them opportunities to earn money at the earliest possible age. Talk to them about the importance of saving and planning. The sooner these concepts take root, the better off your kids will be as adults. Don't feel guilty or ashamed of what you don't have. Making money doesn't make you a good parent, and lack of money doesn't make you a bad one.

Our young teenager, Erik, came to me recently with an idea. He had a dream of someday buying a truck. It was a great opportunity to help him see how financial planning works. I sat down with Erik and asked him four questions: How much would the truck cost? What would he do with it? When did he want to have the money in hand? And how was he going to earn the money? We talked, and his dad and I helped him develop a detailed plan for how he could raise the money and meet his goal.

Don't let money be a secret subject in your household. It's too important for you and for your children.

PROBLEM: Our kids are experts at loading on the guilt and talking me into purchases we can't afford. It's just that I hate to see them go without.

SOLUTION: Don't cave in to your kids.

Moms are especially prone to putting themselves last in financial matters. When they see that another family member needs help or desperately wants something, they may hand out money or buy a gift that ends up being a budget buster. This problem is especially common when kids are involved. "Mom, everybody I know has a [fill in the blank]!" is a frequent plea.

The solution is easier to say than to do. How do you not cave in to your kids? You must set boundaries for your family's expenditures and not let your children put you in a financial bind. Remember, you are their parent: if you start giving in on money issues, you're more likely to give in on other vital, even moral issues. Money is an easy place to draw a line in the sand. I also believe that it's frightening for kids when you give them the power to decide how your family finances will be spent. When we take away their boundaries, we take away their security. Love your kids enough to say no when necessary—and look for opportunities to empower and educate them about the value of a dollar.

We love to say yes to our kids, and you can say yes in more than one way. Not just "Yes, you can have that" but "Yes, you can buy that. It's not in our budget right now, but this is what it costs, and you can earn the money to buy it yourself." Maybe your kids can host a lemonade stand, start a car-wash business, dog-sit, sell baked goods, or do yard work in the neighborhood to earn the money they need. Because of the times we live in, these activities may require adult supervision. Recently, when my daughters, Lily and Chloe, and I left our lemonade stand for a few minutes to begin packing up, someone ran off with our chairs! Yet finding opportunities like this for your children has many benefits. They might discover a hidden talent or passion. They might learn to take pride in their efforts and see the connection between work and wages. Giving in too easily to your kids can actually rob them of their motivation and many valuable lessons.

PROBLEM: In the next five years I'll be sending three kids to college, and I don't know how we're going to pay for it all. What if this completely wipes out our retirement savings?

SOLUTION: Stay committed to your future.

Many parents today are concerned about saving for their children's college expenses, and rightly so. The cost of earning a four-year degree has never been higher. Look into all of the available options, such as 529 college savings plans, scholarships, student loans, and work-study opportunities, and carefully weigh the benefits of more expensive schools against their costs.

If you are forced to choose between funding your kids' college education and sticking to your retirement plan, however, I encourage you to provide for your own needs first. Your children have options, but if your money runs out in your golden years, where will you go for financial help? If you don't take care of your own needs, you'll end up a financial burden to your children.

One way to avoid this distressing scenario is simply to keep working. Too often I've heard about people who retired early but soon found themselves bored and short of funds. The longer you continue in a career, the more your retirement savings, pensions, and potential social security benefits will have to offer you. Face it. If you haven't saved enough, you'll need the income and the mental stimulation. I have a friend who's nearly eighty and starting new businesses regularly. She's never bored. Why not follow her example?

No matter when you plan to retire, it's important to make your retirement program a high priority for savings. When that time finally arrives, your kids will be grateful to learn that you've prepared for your future and they don't have to worry about you.

Money Solutions Checklist

☐ Are you keeping the right attitude about money?

☐ Do you have a budget, and are you sticking to it?

☐ Do you have adequate health, life, home, and auto insurance?

☐ Are you following your retirement strategy?

☐ If you have debt, do you know exactly what you owe and have a plan for paying it off?

☐ Do you have a will, and is it up-to-date?

☐ Do you need to establish a trust fund or living will?

☐ Are you openly discussing money matters with your children and teaching them financial fundamentals?

☐ Are you monitoring the status of your investments and financial commitments?

☐ Are you going online (or consulting other resources) regularly to lessen your fears and expand your knowledge about money?

chapter two

Every Home
Needs Happiness

Lately, it seems like our family time at home

is depressing and tense, just one frustration

after another. What's a better way?

*R*ecently, during a furniture convention at the World Market Center in Las Vegas, our team was having a pretty exciting evening. We were surrounded by friends, family, our manufacturers, and retailers. My friend Erik Estrada was master of ceremonies for the party. My friend Anita Pointer was headlining a concert for us. You can imagine my surprise when she dedicated one of the Pointer Sisters' most exciting songs, "Happiness," to Kathy Ireland Home. My jaw dropped, and it got me to thinking: every home needs happiness.

When you and the rest of your family are happy, your day goes more smoothly, your problems are resolved more quickly, and your life flows like a fresh and beautiful spring. As world champion boxer and entrepreneur George Foreman has said, "You just can't beat ol' happy." Happiness is something we all desperately want and need. In childhood we learn about the Declaration of Independence and the phrase "life, liberty, and the pursuit of happiness." We Americans consider happiness an inalienable right, and we pursue it with passion—but often, sadly, without success.

Happiness seems elusive for many of today's families. We're overwhelmed, underpaid, and under pressure, and the results in many homes are tension and conflict. Too many parents and their kids turn to destructive habits to get through their days: alcohol, drugs, inappropriate sexual activity, overspending, and more. In these as well as less dysfunctional families, bickering is a standard mode of communication. Families turn to counselors, therapists, and church leaders to mediate disputes between husband and wife, parent and child, brother and sister, yet frequently the conflicts remain unresolved. Divorce, to a staggering degree, has become commonplace: more than half of today's marriages break up. In extreme cases, parents physically abuse their children, a terrible tragedy. But are we aware of our kids' vulnerability to emotional abuse? A thoughtless, cruel, or sarcastic comment at an unguarded moment can cripple a young life forever. Both forms of abuse take place every day.

Some time ago I heard a story I will never forget. A woman was describing how miserable her life was with her husband. When asked what she could do to change her circumstances for the better, the woman answered, "I'll never leave, and we'll never be happy, because my revenge on my husband is not complete." This bitter attitude toward life is scary, and it's likely more common than we realize.

What's wrong with us? We may be pursuing happiness, but we're not catching it. Are we sacrificing happiness today because of hurts from yesterday? Are we going to be discontented, or, worse, miserable for the rest of our lives? Do we have to live this way? The answer to that, of course, is no. In fact, you may be surprised how easy it is, after a little strategic thinking, to bring real happiness into your life and home. Keep reading, and I'll explain what I mean.

Defining Happy

By now you've probably asked yourself, "Am I happy?" Before you answer, I suggest you ask yourself another, far more important question: "How do I define 'happy'?" Go ahead, pull out a piece of paper or open up your laptop and record what comes to mind. What does your happiness look like? Feel like? How do you touch it? How do you experience it? Your answers to these questions will be more profound than you might think.

I once was a guest panelist at a speaking event with Barbara Walters and Dr. Maya Angelou, both women I greatly respect. We were speaking at the conference at different times. Ms. Walters made the statement that women can't "have it all." Later, when it was my turn to communicate, I politely disagreed with her. I said that women can have it all but that we may not be able to have it all at the same time. Marriage, career, motherhood, household CEO, commitments to church and other nonprofit organizations, and other life responsibilities are enormous challenges that can drain even the most highly skilled and motivated among us. Trying to fill all of these roles successfully as well as simultaneously is like juggling three balls while riding a bicycle across a tightrope over Niagara Falls. Sure, you might be able to pull it off, but it's far more likely that sooner or later, something will be going over the edge—and it will probably be you!

My point is that you don't need to have it all at the same

moment, with the pressures that go along with that. What does having it all really mean, anyway? Your "all" needs to be just that—yours. You need to define it. Don't allow your perception of someone's fantasy to become your blueprint for living. Your life, like your fingerprints, will be different from someone else's. It's your unique gift from God. For me, that means following the path I believe God has set me on. That path is a wonderful place, where we can be happy.

If you're a mom who's trying to be everything to everyone, are you doing it because it brings you happiness or because it's part of someone else's agenda? As moms we aim to please. We want to meet and exceed the expectations of others, whether they are our children, spouse, friend, neighbor, or our own mother. We may buy into someone else's idea of a successful, happy life without ever really thinking about how it will impact our own. Be careful that you don't let another person's definition of happiness substitute for yours.

Letting go of others' expectations can be extremely freeing. Suddenly you don't have to work crazy hours each week to make payments on a car you don't really need. You don't have to prepare the perfect meal every night—your family will survive the occasional tuna sandwiches and vegetable sticks. You don't have to have every item of clothing washed, folded, and put away at the end of the day. It'll wait until tomorrow. If taking off some pressure gives you greater peace in your heart—and more happiness—then allow yourself the freedom to be less than your image of perfection.

Knowing What's Truly Important

Let's take a look at what you wrote for your personal definition of happiness. Does it match up with the way you're living your life? When can you make changes to move closer to your definition of happiness? Don't put it off until tomorrow—let's start today. If you aren't quite sure how to answer these questions or are simply feeling overwhelmed, make a list of your priorities. What is most important to you? What people and activities and attitudes bring you the greatest joy? Are you thinking "big thoughts" about your life and your future? Do you have a vision for fulfilling your goals? It's tough to be happy if your daily life and priorities aren't aligned. If you spend most of your time focusing on your priorities and passions, you'll probably be much happier.

When I write out my own priorities, my faith in Jesus Christ tops the list. He is my foundation. He is my daily source of purpose and joy. The Bible says, "Consider it pure joy, my brothers, whenever you face trials of many kinds" (James 1:2). We can find joy even when the state of our lives isn't all we're wishing for. Since God wants us to find joy even in our trials and tribulations, I believe He expects us to celebrate the good times even more. That's a great encouragement to me.

One of the little things I do to remind myself about my priorities is to take a sheet of paper and write, in big capital letters, *JOY*. After each letter, I fill in a word: Jesus, Others, You. I keep one of these JOY signs on my bathroom mirror and another in my kitchen. On days when I'm feeling more stressed than joyful, those signs stop me in mid-step. I'll think, *Okay, wait a second . . . maybe I need to rearrange my priorities at this moment.* And when I do that, the joy returns. It's a simple technique, one anyone can use to help remind him or her of what's important. Your list will be different from mine. Whatever it is, keep it in front of you so that your eyes are focused on the prize. The key is to stay attuned to what matters most to you so you can maintain a joyful atmosphere in your life and home.

What matters most to the moms I talk with is time with their families. Kids, especially, change quickly and move into new phases of life. We don't want to miss anything. Our sons and daughters need our guidance and steady presence. They also need us to be happy so we can bring happiness into their lives. Yet unless we are vigilant in protecting our family time, it disappears. It's easy for seemingly important events to intrude on this precious resource.

I remember a wonderful offer that came to me several years ago. I was invited to participate in a short-term project that would pay three times the annual salary I was earning at that point. My advisers thought it was a great opportunity and strongly encouraged me to say yes. The problem was that it was scheduled on the same day as my wedding anniversary, it couldn't be changed, and I'd already made plans with my husband. I'd decided early in my marriage that celebrations on special days such as anniversaries and my husband's and children's birthdays were too important to postpone. I do admit that I have worked on my own birthday, and that's probably not the best boundary. When I considered what to do about the conflict with our anniversary, it was no contest. I turned down the project and enjoyed my time with Greg instead.

Husbands and, even more so, your children, will intuitively sense if they are cherished and if they are your priority. When you set aside other important and pressing issues to make time for them, it sends a message that they are first in your life. You may miss out on a business opportunity, a fun time with a girl-friend, or that haircut you really need. Sometimes you'll even miss out on your daily shower (we moms know that perfume is shower in a bottle). Yet by letting go of other priorities, you'll be honoring your family and cultivating a happy home. In the long run, it will be more than worth the sacrifice of any other opportunity.

The Power of Place

Another key to a happy home is maximizing the impact of our physical environment. For most moms, even if we work outside the home, our house or apartment is our primary "office." For better and worse, it is the space that communicates how we're feeling about ourselves and our lives. Never underestimate the power of place to either lift your spirits or take a toll on your emotional well-being. I urge you to step back and consider how your home is making you feel. Years of living in the same spot can have a numbing effect on your senses. You may not even realize that the atmosphere of your living space is making you tense, anxious, and depressed when it should be leaving you re-laxed, at peace, encouraged, and happy.

You may sense that your physical surroundings are draining your energy but aren't sure why. It could be that your furniture feels hemmed in and out of balance. It's possible that the colors on the walls, which once felt exciting and enlivened your decor, now appear out-of-date, stuck in the past. If your life has changed, why haven't your colors? Or are you overwhelmed by one of the most common culprits of all—clutter? With tons of clutter, you may not be able to even see the colors of your walls.

Is your home filled with things you no longer want or need? Are you hoarding to compensate for or cover up some emotion? Are your tables and floors covered with toys, clothes, dishes, and unread magazines? These are signs that clutter is taking over your life. It's easy to get weighed down by possessions. In some cases, the desire to acquire becomes a disease. People have closets and rooms full of things that weigh them down. If that's your situation, don't hesitate—it's time to act. Attack your home one room at a time. As you come to each item, either put it to use or get rid of it. If it's a ticket from a movie with your kids that evokes a special memory, put it in a scrapbook to preserve the memory, design a Christmas craft with it, or throw it away. Learn to let go. As you do, you'll rediscover the inviting home you once knew and loved.

I don't mean that every item and scrap of paper in your home has to be out of sight. That's certainly not the case in our home. My desk, which used to be my kitchen table, is covered with paperwork. You might call it a mess. Yet I know what each piece of paper is and where it goes. It's an organized mess! So I'm not suggesting that your home has to pass a white-glove inspection. On the other hand, if your bedroom doorway is blocked by boxes of Christmas cards from people you haven't talked to in ten years, it's time to step in and "clutter bust."

I am a firm believer that we are influenced by our environment, usually more than we realize. You may be reluctant to put much energy into transforming your home into a more welcoming place. I understand. However, once you acknowledge the far-reaching impact a positive living space has on your spirit, you can begin making changes for the better. We'll talk in this chapter about how relatively small steps, such as adding a touch of aromatherapy or setting out candles, can make an enormous difference in the atmosphere of your home (it's hard to have arguments by candlelight). We'll discuss fun ideas for displaying personal items that celebrate your unique personality and make you feel comfortable and honored. We'll also explore ways to establish a cozy little nook in your home that is just for you, a private place you can turn to for tranquility.

If you're anything like me, you'll need help—expert help—to make all the changes needed to transform your house into a happy home. I freely admit that cooking and gardening are not among my strengths. That's why I often turn to my good friend Chef André Carthen of ACafe and renowned landscape designer Nicholas Walker of J du J for advice. In this chapter Chef André and Nicholas will offer you solutions for entertaining and for developing a refreshing physical environment outside your home—as well as enabling some of that outdoor refreshment to come inside.

You may not be an expert on kitchen, garden, and living spaces. You are, however, an expert on you and what your family needs. Even if you have limited time and financial resources, with a little bit of help, you can develop a style for your home that reflects who you are and what makes you happy. We'll talk more about that, too. What is crucial is looking for opportunities to allow your surroundings to flourish. It can be the magnet that attracts the joy hidden inside your heart.

Looking for Joy in All the Right Places

We've talked about how many families are pursuing but not finding happiness. Some moms, though, are tired of the chase. They've tried for so long and have become so discouraged that they've given up. They're waiting for someone or something to come along and rescue them. They feel empty. They have a void in their hearts that desperately needs to be filled.

I remember the day one of our children wanted to run away from home. I'd read all the manuals and instruction books that said parents should question the decision but then allow their child to pack. The key was to never let the child see you panic or allow him to think he could intimidate you. Yet when my child was the one announcing plans to run away, my response was the complete opposite of what I'd read. As soon as I heard the words, I dissolved into tears. Not a good example of parenting! So believe me, I do understand how overwhelming, intimidating, and even frightening it can be to have mom responsibilities, and how that can leave mothers with an empty feeling that cries out to be filled.

For me, that void is filled by the Lord. When I take my troubles to Him, I find comfort and strength that give me an inner joy and allow me to keep going even when I'm discouraged by my circumstances. I appreciate that you may not share my faith. If you don't, you won't find your support in the same way

I do. I will tell you this, though: if we wait for happiness, we are likely to find ourselves paralyzed by the waiting.

A mother once wrote to me and said, "I want to be happy. I'm waiting for something to happen to help me be happy." I wrote back and encouraged her to begin moving toward joy that day. We corresponded further, and I urged her to start with simple steps: Organize a junk drawer. Discard things she didn't need. Visit her children at school. Decide that rather than argue with her husband over their differences, she could realize that they each had their own visions for their lives, and she could focus on what they had in common. Today this mom leads a much happier life. She has stopped waiting for happiness to come to her and is starting to look for joy in the right places.

I don't mean to imply that discovering happiness is easy, especially for anyone struggling with genuine depression. Without doubt, there are circumstances and medical conditions that require professional help, including prescription medication. Emotional illness is as real as any physical illness. If you find yourself in a place of depression that you can't break through, or if you're overwhelmed to the point of danger to yourself or another human being, please put this book down immediately and get help. Too often, however, people turn to chemical substitutes—even from our own physicians, who may be quick to prescribe them—rather than attempt to solve the core problem. If you're unhappy, there is much you can do to change your situation. Life is too precious to go through it without joy.

One of the best ways to discover joy is to reach out to others. When we see beyond ourselves and observe the needs of the people around us, we open ourselves and our children up to all kinds of opportunities for joy. Years ago I worked in a convalescent home. It was a pleasure for me to deliver meals to the elderly patients, many of whom had no one else to visit them. Many were not happy. Their health was poor, and they were lonely. Yet the simple act of giving them a smile and hug and of serving them a meal brought heartfelt smiles to their faces. When my shift was done, I felt joy over the fact that basic acts of kindness could cause someone to feel a small difference in their life.

When you reach out to others, the impact goes beyond you and the person you're helping. Imagine the lessons your children will learn if, from an early age, they see you volunteering once a month to read to the blind or serve in a soup kitchen. Better yet, if your kids are old enough, encourage them to volunteer with you. In Santa Barbara we have a program in which we bring flowers to people who otherwise don't have access to them, so that they can experience one of God's wondrous creations. The program serves women and men who have limited mobility or are confined to their living space, including those in convalescent homes. Even people at our local mission, who may be temporarily homeless, benefit from the program and can enjoy the scent and beauty of a flower. This is something we've participated in as a family. I believe our children have learned powerful lessons from seeing firsthand the impact of kindness. No matter how much joy they give out, they receive even more.

I'm not suggesting that you should volunteer at the expense of your family time or your own overwhelmed schedule. It's important to set boundaries and establish what you can and cannot do. Still, when you make it a priority to focus on others, you may find that other, more trivial concerns will begin to fall away.

If you're reading this and thinking that you have very little time or money to give to others right now, I understand that. If you are a person of faith, however, you always have the option to pray. I'm reminded of a time when I learned that two boys at school were bothering one of our children. My first reaction wasn't very loving. I was upset. Later that evening, though, when I calmed down, our child and I prayed for those two boys. Just leaving the matter in God's hands was a blessing. Knowing that He hears and answers every prayer created a sense of peace and happiness for both of us. And the next day I found out that the situation had indeed improved.

Put simply, compassion leads to joy. In the Bible, the apostle Paul wrote, "If you have any encouragement from being united with Christ, if any comfort from his love . . . then make my joy complete by being like-minded, having the same love" (Philippians 2:1–2). Any time that we follow the example of Jesus, we radiate joy. Everyone around us will see it, receive it, and most often, reflect it back.

Beginning Today

You can be happy today. Remember when I said that some people have a void they want someone or something to fill? It's as if they're stuck in an "if, then" mode. If I can just have a baby girl, then I'll be happy. If we can make enough to afford a new house, then I'll be happy. If my boss gives me that transfer

I want, then I'll be happy. They're always waiting for some external event to bring joy into their lives.

You don't have to wait. You can choose happiness right now. God tells us to be patient in our trials and in waiting for the return of Jesus (see Romans 12:12 and James 5:7), but He doesn't say we have to wait for joy. On the contrary, He wants us to always celebrate our lives and faith: "Rejoice in the Lord always. I will say it again: Rejoice!" (Philippians 4:4). Remember Paul and Silas, who were severely flogged and chained to a prison wall (Acts 16:23–24)? They seemed out of options, yet they raised their own spirits and those of their fellow prisoners by offering prayers and hymns to God.

Yes, we will have moments of sorrow in our lives; but real joy isn't based on circumstances. Real joy is something that cannot be taken away. Even in the midst of crisis or grief, deep in our hearts, we have the joy of knowing that we're not alone. We have God, the people we love, and the precious gift of life. No matter what else is going on around us, those are blessings we should never take for granted.

Real Solutions

Of all the techniques that could help "Grumpy" so you can enjoy a happier family life, nothing will be more important than your choice to establish a culture of joy in your home. During my childhood, there were many days when my parents easily could have changed my name to Grumpy. The choice I make to be as positive about every situation as possible did not become a reality for me until I found my faith. My ability to be positive and joyful continues to grow as my faith grows.

My husband and I are excited about serving on the board of a new Christian high school in Santa Barbara. To make sure that everyone is always moving in a Christian direction, our board unanimously committed to establishing a culture of joy as one of the founding principles of the school. We want that attitude to infuse every interaction among students, teachers, and administrators. It sets the tone for educational goals, growth opportunities, accountability standards, and consequences. Love and forgiveness are the models, springing out of a culture of joy.

What's important in an education environment is even more critical at home. One of the best ways to establish a joyful atmosphere for your family is to make the choice to honor one another. We know that Scripture instructs us to honor our parents. In the first book of the Bible, we learn that Noah drank too much wine and was discovered naked in his tent by Ham, his youngest son. Ham's response was to broadcast the news of his father's indiscretion to his two brothers. The older brothers, however, chose to honor their father. They grabbed a garment and walked backward into the tent to avoid disgracing Noah further (Genesis 9:20–23).

We must teach our children to honor and respect their parents, but it's equally vital that we apply this same attitude to our kids. Understand that each son or daughter is an individual with specific, God-given gifts and traits. Pay attention to your kids' unique abilities and characteristics. Help them recognize these qualities in themselves, and commend your children when they demonstrate their talents. If your daughter has an aptitude for math, let her know how pleased and impressed you are with her work. If your son struggles in the classroom but has a knack for playing the trumpet, encourage him to develop his skills. Your support will help your kids feel better about themselves and enable them to see their differences not as faults but as special, valued gifts.

Another way to honor one another is in your choice of words. Words are powerful. Simple statements communicate and convey so much information: yes; no; why; how. Short phrases can set the tone for an entire relationship: thank you; yes, please; you're welcome. I suggest you make a list of positive and negative words and then pay attention to what you say when you greet your kids after school and as you converse. Which kinds of words are you using most of the time? If your daughter has a sour look on her face, are you more likely to say, "Are you okay, honey?" or "What's your problem now?"

Choose words that uplift, celebrate, empower, and encourage. If your son brings home an English report with a grade that disappoints you, are you disappointed for the right reasons? Is it because you know he could have done better or because you think he's making you look bad as a parent? Be careful not to launch into attack mode when your kids don't meet your expectations. Instead of accusing or saying, "How could you do this?" a better approach might be questions such as "How did we get here?" and "What made it hard for you?" Rather than seeking blame, look for ways to foster improvement for the next time. Let your children know that you're not looking to "bust them" but that everyone in the family is on the same team.

You can also help establish a culture of joy by openly admitting your mistakes. Not long ago I was responsible for bringing snacks for our church congregation to munch on after the Sunday service, but when Sunday morning arrived I didn't remember to check my calendar, and I completely forgot about the snacks. At church I realized I'd blown it, and I felt terrible. Yet it was a wonderful lesson for our children (and for me). I was able to share with them how important it is to check their schedules whenever a project is due.

No matter how careful we are as parents, and no matter how many parenting books we read, there will be times when we're just wrong. We all make mistakes. Perhaps you'll give your child an unreasonable grounding, or your bad day at work will translate into an angry response at home. When you make those mistakes, don't be afraid to apologize and ask for forgiveness. Your children will appreciate your honesty, and you'll be teaching them a valuable lesson. You'll find that families who are willing to admit their mistakes live in the happiest homes.

PROBLEM: Our house is loud and chaotic. To unwind after a long day at school, the kids usually run around in the backyard, blast their music, watch TV, or play a video game—sometimes all at the same time. How do you establish a culture of joy with all that noise going on?

SOLUTION: Make a "bubble" for your kids.

A little loud and crazy "unwind time" after school will be a welcome change of pace for many kids, but don't let it dominate the rest of your family's day. Remember, you are the parent! Just as your children need times to run and shout and play, they also need moments of peace to rest and recharge. No matter what the time of day, if you sense that the energy level is about to shoot off the scale, then think about ways you can bring it down to a manageable point. It might be time for the kids to start on their homework. Maybe they need to retreat to their rooms to read or listen to a recorded story. Or maybe you'll want to apply a lesson I learned from a cartoon character. Have you ever seen the Tasmanian Devil spin into a one-creature wrecking crew? The damage that little guy can inflict is amazing. Yet when Bugs Bunny pulls out a violin and begins to play a sweet lullaby, Taz just melts. They say that music soothes the savage beast. It works on Taz, and it works with children, too. It's hard to scream, argue, or throw a tantrum when a wonderful, soothing melody is playing. Give it a try!

Another way to cut down the noise is to develop what I call "bubble" times. In our family, the process of getting our three kids ready and off to school in the morning can be more than a little hectic. We may be running behind, one child may want juice, another might want to play hide-and-seek, and another might want a change of clothes. We'll have some drama and hear more than a few cross words. It's a victory just getting everyone into the car. Maybe you can relate. On those days, by the time we pull out of the driveway, everyone is feeling a bit crabby and frazzled (including Mom).

I have a rule for when we're in the car, though: video games and cell phones, including mine, get turned off. Our drive to school takes about twelve minutes, and for that short period of time, I talk with the kids about what's going on in their lives, what's coming up at school, and what they're thinking about. I try to encourage them about anything they might be struggling with. We might listen to music and talk about why it's enjoyable. Sometimes we'll play word games or guess at how many trees we'll see before we stop. We may look for people who need help; if an ambulance goes by, we'll pray for the person inside. We'll talk about dreams and plans for the future.

Usually, by the time we arrive at school, I'm amazed at the changes that have taken place. Frowns have turned into smiles. Bad moods and worries have faded away, and the kids are ready to tackle a new day. When we're in that bubble, the kids and I are insulated from the world's pressures. It's time for us to focus on one another and build each other up. The more bubble times you can insert into your family's day, the easier it will be to establish a culture of joy.

PROBLEM: I can't stand the look of our home—it leaves me discouraged and just feels wrong. I want to change everything but don't know where to start. How can I do this with a tiny budget?

SOLUTION: Make big changes with a few simple steps.

Our surroundings can have a huge influence on our state of mind, and if we're already discouraged, an oppressive living space will increase our sense of being overwhelmed. Whether it's the lighting, the colors, the clutter, or simply the feeling evoked by a combination of factors, when your home environment doesn't work for you, it's extremely difficult to be happy. Your house or apartment should reflect your heart and your inspiration. It can be a place of daily restoration, where you renew your energy, reinvigorate your senses, and nurture your soul. Here are a few easy and affordable ways to establish a more positive physical environment at home.

- *Wall coverings.* Wall coverings today are not the wallpaper of yesteryear. They bring texture, beauty, excitement, and design influences from around the world to every room. Wall coverings are easier to apply than ever before, and much more affordable. If a large wall-covering project doesn't fit into your budget, try covering just one wall and painting the rest. Pull the colors from your favorite wall covering into the rest of the room.

- *Color.* Beiges and grays can lend consistency to home

decor but may not bring out the feeling of joy you want. Try adding a splash of "God's colors" to your walls: bright and bold yellows, whites, blues, oranges, and greens. Consider what type of paint will best suit your purpose. Flat paint tends to hide imperfections in the underlying surface better than its higher-gloss cousins but is more susceptible to stains. Low-luster finishes, including eggshell and satin, require well-prepared surfaces but are effective for high-use areas because they're easier to clean. Buy all your paint at the same time to ensure uniformity of color and texture, and purchase 10 percent more than what you think you need so that you'll have enough to cover spills and touch-ups in the future.

- *Furniture.* While the color of a room certainly helps determine its warmth, the placement of furnishings also influences the mood. Look at each room in your home and ask yourself: What are the interesting architectural elements? Are there windows, a fireplace, multiple doors? How many people will use this room, and what will they use it for? What are the traffic patterns? Is the room near the front door, or is it tucked away? Once you've answered these questions, determine what the focal point of each room will be, perhaps a fireplace or a lovely picture window. This focal point will help define your space.

  Arrange primary pieces first. Try to mix furniture sizes and heights to create visual interest. Group pieces that relate to one another to connect the room and give it warmth. Case goods, leather, and upholstery all blend together to make living spaces exciting and individual. And if you work at home, as I often do, consider investing in furniture that is especially for your home office. It really makes a difference in your commitment and organization.

- *Flooring.* If you have the resources to install new flooring, you can bring fresh elegance and functionality to a room. Hardwood is still at the top of many lists, but the affordability and durability of today's laminate and tile surfaces also make these a popular choice. Carpet, too, is a powerful decor element. It adds comfort and insulation and is available in a variety of colors, styles, and textures. When it comes to luxurious softness underfoot, nothing surpasses carpet. Remember to carefully consider how your room will be used before adding a floor surface that will be there for years.

  For a dramatic change that won't break your budget, consider an area rug. It can change the feel of a room in an instant and look great over neutral carpet, on traditional hardwood, or on any ceramic style. By selecting an area rug with colors that are present in the surrounding decor, your room's "fifth wall"—the floor—can pull everything together.

  Remember that light-colored rugs make a room seem airy, while darker styles establish an intimate feeling. If you're looking to create a focal point, opt for bold colors and ornate designs. If your rug's purpose is to quietly complement the existing design, a solid color or subtle pattern works best. In a room with heavy traffic, a solid, dark rug is most effective for disguising wear and tear.

- *Home enhancements.* If a room in your home feels cold and uninteresting or just plain drab, look to the light. A combination of the three basic types of lighting—ambient, task, and decorative—will give a room a sense of cohesion while also making it comfortable and functional.

Ambient, or background, lighting envelops a room in a soft, warm glow and eliminates harsh contrasts between bright and dark areas. Try installing a dimmer switch on individual fixtures for maximum flexibility.

Task lighting is especially effective for reading, writing, cooking, grooming, or any activity that requires high visibility and attention to detail. Lighting levels can vary but should begin at a minimum of sixty watts.

Decorative lighting is valued more for its appearance than its usefulness. You might incorporate decorative lighting by adding low-wattage accent lights to potted plants. Small lights can have a dramatic impact by illuminating foliage and casting shadows on the wall. Try adding a pair of decorative sconces on either side of a doorway, and you'll be impressed with the simple yet elegant effect.

You'll find that many other home enhancement options seem minor but can deliver an entirely new feeling to your home. A new window covering—wood, aluminum, or vinyl horizontal blinds; vinyl or fabric vertical blinds; pleated or honeycomb shades; or roller shades—can enhance a room's look.

Beautiful bed linens will invite you to relax and refresh. Feel free to mix stripes and plaids if the colors go well together, and remember that masses of pillows add a luxurious quality. From babies to tweens, choose bed linens that celebrate the personality of the loved one who's sleeping there. A quality mattress will help you get a good night's sleep.

For zero maintenance other than dusting, permanent botanicals are an excellent solution. A water feature such as an indoor fountain, whether small or large, cleans the air and is soothing on the nerves. An air purifier or humidifier can also help keep the air in your home fresh and free from pollutants. A ceiling fan is another way to keep the air in your home moving. It will provide relief during hot summer days and, depending on the style you choose, add a touch of the elegant or exotic to your decor.

• *Accessories.* Whether you're five or a hundred and five, you've acquired a collection of items that appeal to you. One of my sisters collects fine porcelain. She made me aware of the company that makes it, and I fell so in love with their work that I began designing collections for them. Use accessories to add personality to your home and to tell a story about yourself to guests. Strive for balance in your display. Symmetrical arrangements are equal on both sides of a central line and establish a more formal look. If your pieces vary in size, shape, and color, try a more informal, asymmetrical look.

Group similar items together and in odd numbers; displays of three and five work well. Arrange everything around one focal point. Create depth by zigzagging or alternating pieces from back to front instead of placing them a straight line. Bring together items of different textures for a unique look. For example, if you have a grouping of brass candlesticks and a ceramic vase, try adding a plant, floral arrangement, or woven basket for a softer texture. Consider a wall arrangement, but remember to experiment before you start hammering nails. Don't be afraid to try something different. What's important is that your accessories satisfy you.

- *Aromatherapy.* One of the easiest ways to turn your home into a retreat is to engage your most instinctual sense, the sense of smell. Fill your home with scented candles, herbal sachets, potpourri, diffusers, and bowls of dried flowers to achieve a therapeutic effect. Many moms have told me that on those rare evenings alone, a candle has been their comfortable companion, helping provide a much-needed sense of peace. You can also employ essential oils—concentrates of flowers, plants, and woods that, when released individually or in specific combinations, have a positive effect on your psyche—by putting a few drops in your bathroom soap dispenser or on your furnace's air filters. Try naturally calming scents like lavender and vanilla in your bedroom.

- *Personal space.* You'll feel so much better about your home and life if you have a special, private place to retreat to for the sole purpose of nurturing your spirit. Whether this space is an extra bedroom, the attic, or a partitioned corner at the back of your living room, it should evoke a soothing sense of peace and harmony. This space should be thought of as a refuge from the world and from household obligations. You may want to furnish it with your favorite things; position a comfortable chair and ottoman near a window; add a cozy throw, a place for a cup of tea, and a book you've always wanted to read. Give yourself permission to regularly spend an uninterrupted hour reading, thinking, praying, or daydreaming. Whatever you decide, remember that this is your time to refresh. Enjoy it!

- *Design.* Many moms tell me that they wish they could craft an overall look and feel for their home. Even if they don't have the opportunity to travel, they have a sense—from the Internet, watching television, and reading books and magazines—of certain themes that capture their interest. Our design philosophy at KIWW is based on eight style guides we've developed from talking with mothers and from our own observations and travels: *Aloha, Americana, Architectural, European Country, Far East Dreams, Ivory Coast, In Russian Style,* and *La Vida Buena.* Every product we design, from jewelry to socks to home and skin care, lives and is inspired by our style guides.

Establishing a unified design for your home can be easier and more affordable than you might think. First, identify the look that is most likely to make you happy and excited over a period of years. Then make a room-by-room wish list of items that will help establish the style you want. Determine the cost for each, and prioritize them according to your budget and which rooms are used most. Be willing to consider shopping at garage and estate sales and thrift stores to keep your expenses down. Be patient, and stay within your budget. It won't happen overnight, but if you start today, your dream home can become a reality.

PROBLEM: I admit it—I'm overwhelmed. We have marriage issues, child issues, financial issues, and the house is a total disaster. Some days I'm so discouraged I can barely get out of bed. To me, right now, the idea of being happy sounds like a fairy tale. Help!

SOLUTION: Keep a positive perspective, and take small steps.

An old Italian proverb says, "Without hope, the human heart will surely die." Don't let your heart die—there is hope! I understand what it's like to feel overwhelmed by motherhood. I can't think of any job that is more important and rewarding—or more demanding and challenging—than raising children. It's huge. It's heroic.

To keep that challenge in perspective, it is vital to take a long-range view of your circumstances. Every phase of life is a season, and even though it can be hard to imagine at the time, each one does pass. Ask yourself these simple questions: Am I doing my best as a wife and mother? Do my husband and children know that I love them and am committed to being there for them? Despite the inevitable missteps, am I training our kids to move in a direction that matches our family's priorities? If so, you're probably doing a far better job of managing your life and family than you give yourself credit for. Even if you're not winning the battle today, you're probably still winning the war.

On those mornings when you wake up and don't think you can face another day, remember that the sun will rise tomorrow. Simply listing a few things you have to be thankful for at that moment can be surprisingly encouraging. Maybe your list is as basic as the children you've been blessed with, that there's food in the refrigerator, that you have a friend or two who seem to appreciate you. The Bible encourages us to think about "whatever is true, whatever is noble, whatever is right, whatever is pure, whatever is lovely, whatever is admirable" (Philippians 4:8). Give yourself a few minutes each day to remember the good things in your life. We can find happiness in even the darkest times if we stop to look for it.

When we feel disheartened and overwhelmed, it's as if we're going through life with sunglasses on. The world appears dark and muted. We can't really see the beautiful landscapes that God has painted, the bright blue skies, velvet green grasses, rich brown fields, and sparkling sapphire oceans. It reminds me of the words from one of the great songs performed by wonderful friends of ours, Marilyn McCoo and Billy Davis, Jr., when they were in the vocal group the Fifth Dimension: from the musical *Hair,* "Aquarius/Let the Sunshine In." If we make a conscious effort to take off those dark glasses and open our eyes and hearts, the sunshine *can* pour through. We can appreciate not only the physical beauty of God's creation but also the acts of love and kindness that surround us when we take time to notice. When your focus is off of yourself and on the people and blessings bestowed by God, you can't help moving closer to joy.

Another suggestion, if you often wake up feeling overwhelmed, is to make a list of what you'd like to accomplish that day or even during the next couple of hours. Keep it short and realistic. There are only twenty-four hours in a day, and you can't expect to solve all your problems quickly. By dividing your tasks into small, bite-sized pieces, you'll find it easier to tackle your trials without getting discouraged.

Especially when our three children were younger, there were days when the challenges seemed more frequent than the successes. I believe that half the battle is won when you accept that those days will occur and are prepared for them. We don't live in a fairy-tale world; we live in the real world, so expect the unexpected. Here are a few more simple solutions that can help provide the peace you and the rest of your family need:

- Find a mom who needs help as much as you do, and take turns watching all the kids for a morning or evening. It's amazing what two free hours can do to raise your spirits.

- Have your children—no matter how old they are—do a "stop and clean" fifteen minutes. Gather everyone up, make some quick assignments, set the kitchen timer, and yell "Go!" You'll be surprised at how much can be accomplished in a short time. A simple reward, such as a family game of Uno, will make this fun for kids instead of a chore.

- Seek marriage mentoring or counseling at your local church. Most churches have something like this in place to help couples over the bumps and rough patches in life. Stop problems early in your marriage; don't let them fester.

- If you truly can't shake an overwhelming sense of distress or anxiety, let your family physician know your concerns. It's important to take action. To be the best mom you can be, your family needs you healthy and happy.

PROBLEM: I used to be an organized person, with everything it its place. Now that I have children, our house is a jumbled mess. I forget appointments and can't find anything. Who can be happy living like this?

SOLUTION: Find an organizational system that works for you, and take charge!

I've always been blessed with a good memory. Years ago I might've been sitting in a business meeting, discussing important figures and dates, and one of my partners would say to me, "Aren't you going to write that down?" "No," I'd answer, "it's okay. I've got it." I had no trouble remembering minute details, such as the birthday of a kindergarten classmate who wasn't even a friend. As soon as our son was born, however, my life changed drastically. My duties increased about a hundred times over, and I realized it was no longer safe for me to trust my memory. I was responsible for more than my own life. Something had to change. I needed a system.

For me, the system that works (at least most of the time) is a calendar on our refrigerator with huge squares for each day, leaving lots of room to write down my appointments and all the various commitments of our family. It's simple, and it's in one highly visible place, so when Lily's tennis lessons shift, we all can see the changes on the calendar. I supplement this with sticky notes—lots of them. I've got them on my coffee pot, my telephone, and especially in my car. Sometimes the inside of my car looks like it was attacked by a paper tornado. It's not very high-tech, but for me it usually does the job. Even with that system, I admit that sometimes balls still get dropped. With three young lives to juggle along with my personal and professional responsibilities, things don't always get done perfectly or exactly on time. Most of the time, though, our calendar/sticky-note technique keeps us organized and on schedule.

Everyone is unique, so this approach may not work as well for you and your family. You might prefer to carry a day planner or take advantage of a laptop computer and schedule planner software. Whichever way you choose, it's critical that you have some kind of system that is effective for you and your family in keeping track of your commitments and responsibilities. If you find that you're missing meetings because your memory isn't what it used to be, think about enhancing your current system or adopting a new one. Organization is key to a happy home.

Another important part of getting organized is addressing clutter. Before you know it, your home can fill up with things you don't want, don't use, and don't need. All this stuff takes up physical and mental space. It crowds your living area and causes stress and a sense of chaos. You may not want to face it, but you'll be happier if you do. It's time to clear out the clutter.

We have a system at our company for e-mail that we call DDD: Do It, Delegate It, or Ditch It. Delegate does not mean passing the buck—it means giving it to someone who will do something with it. This is an effective system for work and home. Set aside a day or a weekend, or even a week if needed, and enlist the rest of your family to help with this project. Go room by room and identify what can be recycled, what can be given to a charity or family in need, and what should be tossed. The adage "If in doubt, throw it out" definitely applies here. If you have the ambition to host a garage sale, go for it. You'll be reducing the clutter and making money at the same time.

Once you get your home spruced up, don't stop there. Put systems into place that will help prevent you from falling back into clutter chaos. Storage is a key issue. Our kids, for instance, bring home finished homework and notes from their teachers nearly every day. So that we don't get buried in an avalanche of paper, each child made and painted a wooden file holder in the shape of a house. We keep these in our kitchen, and every afternoon the new papers go into their respective houses, ready for me to read when I have a minute to sit down. Plastic tubs that can be tucked in a closet or under a bed are another great way to organize and store papers and items you don't need every day. I know a mom with four children who, to save space, photographs her kids' school projects and artwork and stores it all on CDs. It's a great solution for keeping cherished memories while saving space.

It's also so important to teach your children how to clean and organize. You can help them by adding hat and shoe racks to their rooms and putting up shelves for toys and games. Devise a simple daily checklist for maintenance. If two children share a room, divide it with an imaginary line and assign each child the responsibility of keeping his or her portion tidy. The sooner you develop good cleaning habits in your children, the sooner you'll have the help you need to develop an orderly, happy home.

PROBLEM: I'm so busy with work and other commitments that I don't spend much time with my kids; but when I am with them, I try to make the most of it. Isn't quality time more important than quantity?

SOLUTION: Strive for quantity *and* quality time.

It's true that the quality of your interaction with your children is extremely important. If you work outside the home, your family time will be even more limited, so it's crucial that you spend it wisely. Make face-to-face bonding time with your children a daily priority. That means time when you're not distracted by household chores or phone calls, or lost in a cloud of work-related worry. This is your chance to focus on your children and find out what's happening in their lives: ask about school, read together, laugh, wipe away tears, and enjoy one another's company. Let your kids know that your time with them is sacred and something that they can depend on.

As important as quality time is with your kids, though, I believe that quantity is just as significant. We cannot expect our kids to open up and share with us on our timetable. Those moments occur during the "nothing" times when you're sitting on the floor doing a puzzle together or just hanging out. Our son, Erik, after finishing his homework in the evening, will often sit down in the kitchen with a bowl of cereal. I've learned that this is his time to talk and it is one of my best opportunities for connecting with him. Even if we moms are tired and have other things on our minds, it is crucial that we make ourselves available at such moments. That can only happen if we're there.

When your children do begin to open up, allow them the space to express themselves. Show that you take them, their moods, and their opinions seriously. Their opinions will often differ from yours. That's okay—agree to disagree. It's more important to keep communication channels open than always to convert your kids to your point of view. Be quick to listen, slow to speak, and slow to become angry. God doesn't make mistakes. He gave us two ears and one mouth because we need to be listening twice as much as we're talking. You'll create a more inviting and joyful atmosphere in your home if you allow your kids to fully convey their feelings and concerns; and they'll be more receptive to your response when they know you've patiently heard and considered their thoughts.

LANDSCAPE DESIGNER
NICHOLAS WALKER OF J DU J
Enjoy a Touch of Nature

For mothers and families looking to bring more happiness into their lives, there's nothing like a touch of nature to enhance their joy. When parents and children experience the variety and beauty of God's creation, they can't help developing a deeper appreciation for their environment and each other.

Establishing and maintaining a kids' garden, for example, is a project that can be easy and fun for everyone. You might dig out a small bed in a sunny area, then let your children sow seeds of lettuce or radishes in a pattern that forms their initials. Try a germinating seed pack, and watch nature unfold. It's also fun to put in a birdbath—it might feature an elaborate design or be a simple bowl—that will attract butterflies, ladybugs, birds, and pollinators, helping you establish your own little ecosystem.

Hardy air plants, which absorb what they need through the air rather than their roots, are a great option for people who don't have a green thumb. They can tolerate long periods without water and can be placed in or on nearly anything. One popular choice is to hang them on fishing line.

Not everyone, of course, has the option of an outdoor garden. If you live in an apartment or are intimidated by the idea of a garden project, why not bring the outdoors in? Here are a few basic ideas that everyone in the family can participate in and enjoy:

- *Compost.* Place a stainless steel pot next to your kitchen sink. Instead of throwing out your lettuce tops, carrot tops, coffee grounds, and eggshells, drop them into your pot. Put those into a compost heap in your backyard—a square area three feet by three feet, held together by wooden slats or wire mesh, is ideal. Gather "brown" materials such as newspapers, leaves, sawdust, and dry yard waste; mix them with the "green" waste from your steel pot (one part green to two parts brown); and turn regularly with a pitchfork. You'll soon have organic nutrients you can use to nourish and replenish your garden.

- *Herbs.* Herbs are easy to grow and require little more than good draining soil, sunlight, and water. To get started, all you need is a flower pot or window box, soil, and the herb of your choice. Your options run from basil to yarrow and everything in between and will enhance all manner of culinary treats.

- *Water.* Bringing water into your home—for example, with an indoor fountain—can add visual interest, help purify the air, and provide restful ambient noise. Let your kids help you decide what and where, and it will become a project the whole family will appreciate.

CHEF ANDRÉ CARTHEN OF ACAFE
Keep Party Planning Fun and Easy

I've seen it happen too often at parties and other events—everyone present has a good time . . . except the host. That person, often a mother, has felt so much pressure to plan and implement a great evening for her guests that for her, the joy is lost. I'm here to say that, Mom, you don't have to do it all. You should enjoy your party, too!

With that message in mind, here are a few tips on making your party planning easy and fun for all, host included.

1. Know your theme. Whether it's a birthday celebration, brunch, cocktail party, holiday get-together, or dinner event, this is the place to start.

2. Choose a time and location. During summertime, a casual outdoor gathering can capture the mood perfectly. When the holidays arrive, indoor elegance may be the preferred choice.

3. Decide on the number of guests. If you're inviting a crowd, you may want to consider a location other than your home. This works especially well for a kids' party—someone else sets up, you simply show up, and someone else cleans up. But for a personal, welcoming feel, nothing beats your home.

4. Stick to your budget. Especially when it's a small party, don't be afraid to ask your guests for help. If one couple brings drinks and another dessert, you can concentrate on the main entrée. When you're shopping at the grocery store, know what's on sale, and remember to look down. The more expensive, brand-name items are placed at eye level. You'll find generic brands near the floor that are often just as good, as well as organic options that are healthier and priced more reasonably than their well-known counterparts. And for your best produce buys, watch for fruits and vegetables that are in season.

5. Select your menu. This will be based on all of the above. Again, keep your choices as stress-free as possible. If you already know how to prepare a great chicken dish or meat lasagna, make that, and (if it's in your budget) order the dessert. Or pick up a roasted chicken or deli items at the market and just make your salad. If it's a children's event, consider fun foods that aren't too fattening, such as baked French fries. You might have the kids make their own mini bagel pizzas. If it's the holiday season, you could set up a gingerbread cookie station and let kids decorate throughout the evening. Think about presenting a rainbow of colors in your menu—it will appeal to the eye and provide a healthy range of choices.

Another point to remember: a good party should awaken all your senses. Consider scented candles and diffusion sticks. Look for bold, attractive (and affordable) visual displays that come right from your home—say, seashells from your daughter's room, or pine cones or the branch of a maple tree from your backyard. Napkins and place settings can have an elegant feel both visually and in your fingers. Your choice of music can add just the right touch to your occasion. This is an opportunity to be creative while keeping it fun.

Finally, invite your family to help you prepare for your big event. Your children, for instance, might help you pick out ingredients for the salad. If they're old enough, they can assist you in gathering visual elements, preparing table settings, and arranging finger foods. The more they participate, they more you'll all enjoy getting ready. Whatever your event, just remember that you don't have to do it all. Entertaining that's fun and easy is always the best way to go.

Happiness Solutions Checklist

☐ Are you living by your definition of *happiness* and not someone else's?

☐ Do you know what your priorities and passions are, and are you pursuing them?

☐ Are you experiencing joy through your physical environment?

☐ Is discouragement or depression holding you back? If so, what can you do about that today?

☐ Is your home environment a culture of joy?

☐ How are you honoring one another in your family?

☐ Are you setting aside peaceful "bubble times" for your family?

☐ Are you keeping a proper perspective on the many challenges of parenting?

☐ Are you spending both quality and quantity time with your children?

☐ Do you really listen to your kids and take action on what you hear?

chapter three

Your Healthy Home

Every year our family resolves to get healthier,

but somehow we never seem to find the time

and motivation. How can I take better care

of my family and myself?

A few years ago a family I know endured a terrible tragedy. The father (to protect their privacy, I'll call him "John") was a forty-two-year-old loving husband, father of three, and man of faith. He was also a busy and successful restaurateur. John was flying home to Southern California after a business trip and felt chest pains and shortness of breath. From his car in the airport parking lot, he called a doctor-friend. "You're having a heart attack," the friend said. "Don't wait to go to the hospital, and don't try to drive yourself. Take an aspirin and call 911."

John was prepared. He did have aspirin in his car, and he took one before calling 911. Within minutes paramedics arrived, stabilized him, and loaded him into an ambulance. He had suffered a massive coronary, but one paramedic told him he'd be fine. John was frightened but confident. He even felt well enough to call his wife and ask her to meet him at the hospital. Just as he arrived, however, John suffered a second major heart attack. The paramedics battled valiantly and did their best, but when they wheeled John out of the ambulance, he was dead.

John was lean and had no prior symptoms of heart trouble.

However, postmortem tests showed that his triglycerides were high, his C-reactive protein levels were through the roof, and multiple arteries to his heart were clogged. John didn't eat too much, but apparently he didn't always eat well, didn't make enough time for exercise, and didn't know the true status of his heart health.

This story was a wake-up call for me. On the surface, John's health seemed fine. He led a full and active life. Beneath the surface, however, the situation was not at all what it seemed. He would have been shocked to see a video of what was going on inside his body. It made me wonder what a video of my insides would show.

Not long after John's death, I received a second wake-up call. I was immersed in work at one of our furniture shows in Las Vegas. During a rare break, I sat down with a cup of coffee and a cookie. One of my partners joined me and suggested that perhaps I needed to take better care of myself. I admit that I became a little defensive. Well, maybe more than a little. "I'm very busy," I said. "My focus right now is on being a mom and running this business. I just don't have the time."

You've probably said something similar as you've driven past the local gym or someone jogging in your neighborhood. Let me remind you of what my partner reminded me: At the beginning of every plane trip, flight attendants instruct us to put on our own oxygen masks before we try to put one on someone else. We can't help others—our husbands, our children, our friends—if we're incapacitated ourselves.

These two incidents forced me to ask myself some tough questions: Am I willing to let my schedule take me away from our children in this life? Is my work worth the risk of leaving

Greg a single parent? Who will help him care for our children if I'm not around? What is truly important?

Healthy living is a huge challenge for busy moms. We're pulled in a thousand different directions, and usually every one of those tugs feels critically important. After our son, Erik, was born, I had the opportunity to make a series of fitness videos. The program I used helped me lose the pounds I had gained from my pregnancy and to maintain a comfortable fitness level. I even went back to school and became a certified fitness instructor. My life routines soon changed, however. Our daughter Lily was born, and our business became more successful and expanded. Then our second daughter, Chloe, was born, and we were even busier personally and professionally. Suddenly, taking time to exercise or plan healthy meals for my husband and me seemed like a luxury I could no longer afford. Our eating, sleeping, and waking schedules were focused around the children's needs. I barely had time to brush my teeth.

Too often, a twenty-four-hour day doesn't seem nearly enough. When your schedule is beyond full, other family needs tend to take precedence over your own. Taking the time to take care of yourself may feel selfish—but it's not. Remember, you have to put on your own oxygen mask first. It's the best thing you can do for your family.

Food for Thought

After my twin wake-up calls, I also realized I didn't know as much about nutrition as I should. I had to do a little research.

For example, I'd always thought of filet mignon as a fancy, expensive, and fattening diet choice. I might have been right about the first two, but I was surprised to learn that filet mignon, cut from the tenderloin, is actually one of the leanest steak cuts one can buy.

If you're not a nutrition expert either, it may be time for you to get more familiar with the famous food pyramid. You might be surprised to see how much it's changed from the one you studied in school. In 2005 the U.S. Department of Agriculture released MyPyramid, a revised food guidance system. It features an emphasis on grains, vegetables, fruits, milk products, and meat and beans. The guidelines recommend following a varied diet, eating in moderation, and making sure physical activity is part of your health plan. The new pyramid program also offers tips on how to personalize your plan. You can learn more about the USDA recommendations at www.mypyramid.gov.

From my perspective, getting into a regular routine of healthy eating is much more effective than looking for a quick fix through dieting or other methods. I know there are many wonderful diets out there that help people lose weight. Yet too often I've watched friends and family members who struggle with weight issues shift from one diet to another, searching for the magic solution. They never seem to find it. Some pounds lost, even more pounds gained, and on to the next "quick fix."

I like balance. I believe you're much better off setting a realistic goal of losing a pound or two a week than relying on a crash-weight-loss program that may be difficult to maintain over the long haul and injurious to your health. I also believe that nutrition without treats is a boring way to live. The minute you declare a specific food or dessert off limits, of course you're going to want it, crave it, demand it. That's how we respond to deprivation. It's imperative not to overindulge, but if you can take a small serving of something sugary and delicious (unless your doctor vetoes it because of diabetes or other health conditions), enjoy it, and stop there—and if you combine those occasional treats with consistent, healthy food choices—then you're going to be fine.

I am pleased that our society is gaining a clearer understanding of the dangers caused by overeating and obesity. Researchers estimate that one-third of children in the United States are either overweight or obese. Stephanie Nano, an Associated Press writer, reported that "increasing numbers of obese children are being diagnosed with type 2 diabetes, high blood pressure, bad cholesterol and other obesity complications that were seldom seen in children before."[1] When people have not just one but several of these medical problems, the diagnostic term is *metabolic syndrome*. You'll want to learn more about metabolic syndrome than we can share with you in this book. Please understand that it's real and that it's dangerous. It is important that you educate yourself about it. Metabolic syndrome frequently goes undiagnosed, but it is a growing and terrible problem.

The obesity crisis deserves the attention it receives. Equally distressing, however, is the growing number of people who are too thin. The modeling industry has long seen people, male and female, starve themselves to achieve an unnatural size and shape; but the problem now affects ordinary families throughout society. Children as young as six years old suffer from anorexia. Compulsive eating and anorexia are flip sides of the same coin—both involve unhealthy relationships with food. If you suspect that you or someone you love is battling an eating disorder, please seek the help you need. Many counseling programs are available to help people work through these difficult issues.

While the origins of eating disorders are complex, and I don't presume to suggest I have all the answers, I do know this: the temporary pleasure derived from adding or subtracting calories will never fulfill you for long. Your happiness will ultimately have to come from a deeper source. For me, it comes from my relationship with God, my family, and being of service to others. That may also be true for you, or your happiness may spring from another life priority. Either way, that's the place to keep your focus—regardless of your calorie count.

Leading the Active Life

First Lady Laura Bush is an amazing woman, and not just because she was patient and kind to me when one of our children had a meltdown during a holiday visit to the White House. I admire many of her qualities and am inspired by her commitment to promoting good health for women. Through her involvement in the Heart Truth campaign and National Wear Red Day, she has spread the message that heart disease is the leading killer of women in America, taking more lives each year than all forms of cancer combined.

In fact, I've had the opportunity to meet and spend time with Laura Bush and Hillary Clinton, two incredibly busy women who have made a priority of taking care of their hearts and themselves.

They understand that being active isn't the same thing as being healthy. These are women who have become knowledgeable about nutrition and have put regular exercise into their routine. No matter what our political affiliations, I'm sure we can all agree that taking care of our bodies is of prime importance.

One of the best ways to give yourself the gift of a healthy heart and achieve overall fitness is with physical activity. We've all heard that, we all know that—now, really, how do we make the change? It's like the Nike slogan: "Just do it." There's no escaping it. Every day of procrastination is a day of danger. If consistent exercise isn't part of your routine, think about the sports and activities you most enjoy. Walking is one of my favorite exercises. Any physical activity with our children is a great joy. I also love to bike, hike, swim, and surf. Regular, organized programs aren't as exciting to me as finding fun things I can do that incorporate physical activity. A program such as aerobic dancing may work great for you. Find whatever it is that you enjoy and are likely to stick with, and make a plan for including it in your lifestyle.

Maybe you can walk or bicycle to the mailbox or post office instead of driving. Maybe you could take two mornings a week to swim at the local athletic club or public pool or to jog around the school track, something I've done with my family. Gardening is another great activity that provides cardiovascular benefits.

If you start with just three ten-minute exercise sessions each week, you can quickly get into a routine. Then start expanding your activity to fifteen or twenty minutes per session, and you'll soon notice welcome and wonderful changes. You'll feel better, you'll sleep better, and you'll be strengthening your heart.

Now that I'm on the sunnier side of forty, I've learned that stretching is also important. I've long had problems with my posture. I tend not to stand up straight. I also have recurring issues with the knee I injured years ago in my skiing accident. And with all the running around I do as a mom, often carrying a child on my back, I've discovered that performing regular stretching exercises relieves much of the stress I put on my body. Incorporate a few minutes of stretches into each day, maybe in the morning or just before bedtime, and you'll soon be more limber and less likely to strain muscles. You can find a variety of effective stretching exercises online, and many excellent DVDs are available. Check them out and choose the exercises and programs that work best for you.

As you strive to improve your overall fitness, remember to tone your upper body. If we don't exercise, as we get older our arms begin to lose their muscle tone. Upper body strength is important for many reasons besides vanity. I remember a time when I was pregnant and driving alone. While waiting at a stoplight, I saw someone who made me feel uncomfortable. Something about this man raised my level of concern. I locked the doors (something I always do now when I'm with our children), but I realized that might not be enough. *What if he tries to get into my car?* I thought. *I have a child to defend now. Am I physically able to protect him?* I decided I needed to make some changes in my exercise routine. I've found that a few modified pushups each day are a great way to enhance upper body strength. Developing lower body strength and flexibility will also add to your feeling fit and physically equipped to deal with an emergency, and then you'll discover another wonderful benefit: greater peace of mind.

By eating well and adopting or continuing a physical fitness program, you'll be doing more than keeping your body in shape. You'll also be a good role model for the rest of your family. This is important. Because of the dangers of today's world, our children don't have the same opportunities we had to run and play unsupervised and burn off energy. Showing them how to make healthy choices in what they eat and how they exercise increases the likelihood that they'll carry those habits into their adult years. When it's time to cook a meal or prepare a salad, invite your kids into the kitchen and ask them to help choose ingredients or, if they're old enough, chop up the carrots and celery. Likewise, when planning an outdoor family event or vacation, give your children the opportunity to choose some of the physical activities. When they have a vested interest in your meals or vacation agenda, they'll be more likely to embrace them.

As you strive to improve your own and your family's health, you will, of course, run into obstacles. Don't let that discourage you! I remember my first visit to an aerobics class and how excited I was to be doing something about my fitness. For me, it turned out to be harder than it looked—I had trouble keeping up with the instructor. I wasn't the only one who noticed. When the class was over, someone mentioned that my clumsiness was throwing off the other students. Talk about humiliating! I left that room feeling like a klutz and a failure and questioning whether the struggle to be healthy was worth it. Yet in my heart, I knew that it was—for my sake and for my family's sake. I decided to focus on other exercises I enjoyed, such as hiking, biking, and swimming. Years later, when I was certified as a fitness instructor, I thought back on that embarrassing experience and was able to laugh. I'm just grateful that I didn't give up. You shouldn't either.

Maintaining good health, like staying on top of your finances, is a continual balancing act. It's easy to fall down once in a while. That's okay as long as you get right back up. You may have a bad day and eat too much. You may have a bad week and go off your exercise program. But if you renew your commitment for the long term and get back into your routine, you're much more likely to enjoy a good month, a good year, and a good life.

Don't Delay—See Your Doctor Today

You already know that my husband, Greg, is an emergency-room physician. As you can imagine, our friends much prefer to see him in social settings rather than when he's on duty. The fact is that none of us loves visiting the doctor. We'd rather put off all that poking and prodding to another day, thank you very much. Yet the reality is that regular checkups can mean the difference between minor inconveniences now and heartache later. I urge you to schedule that physical you've been putting off and to keep that mammogram appointment.

Years ago, I did a series of fitness tips for NBC's *Today* show, where I worked with anchor Katie Couric. I later admired Katie's bravery during the tragedy of losing her husband to colon cancer. She began a bold campaign to encourage people to get screened and to help them understand that other than lung cancer, colon cancer takes more lives (female and male) in the United States each year than any other cancer. Yet with early screening, colon cancer is preventable. It's vital that we stay on top of this for ourselves and our spouses. Medical guidelines suggest a first colonoscopy at age fifty. Many people choose to start earlier.

Your husband may want to put off that prostate exam and PSA test his doctor keeps talking about too. Don't allow him to neglect his health. Too much is at stake to delay.

I've already mentioned the dangers of heart disease. It's highly advisable to monitor your cholesterol (good and bad) and triglyceride numbers and take steps to keep them at healthy levels. Another valuable but less well-known test is a procedure that measures your C-reactive protein levels. This is another excellent indicator of whether you need to be concerned about heart and coronary artery disease. Work with your doctor to decide what tests you need, how often you should be tested, and whether any lifestyle changes are in order. Don't be afraid to ask questions! When it comes to your health and your heart, knowledge is your greatest asset.

Finally, please remember that the typical heart attack does not begin with a person in great pain clutching his or her chest, as often portrayed in movies. It's more common to feel discomfort or pressure in the center of the chest that may go away and then return; discomfort or pain in one or both arms, the back, neck, jaw, or stomach; shortness of breath; nausea or light-headedness; or simply more fatigue than usual. Men, in particular, tend to wait for these symptoms to go away and are reluctant to call 911. If you or your husband is experiencing chest discomfort, especially combined with any of these other signs, don't wait—call 911 and get help immediately.

Is Your Home a Drug-Free Zone?

Any conversation about good health should address the topics of alcohol and drugs. I am not opposed to the consumption of alcohol, and I certainly don't presume to tell people whether they should or should not drink. It's a personal decision. I recognize that many people drink responsibly and have no problems with alcohol. In some cases, I have watched alcohol take a terrible toll on people I love. It's not a matter I take lightly.

Many years ago I participated in a marketing campaign for a beer company. My business partners thought it was a wonderful campaign; it also happened to be my only regular income at the time. One of my business partners, who was and still is in an alcohol recovery program, said that the campaign wouldn't cause him to take a drink. The beer company was willing to fund a major "Know when to say when" campaign as part of its marketing efforts. The more I thought about it, though, the more the entire idea just didn't sit well with me. My image was being used to promote beer, a product that does not lead to good health and, in some cases, damages lives and families. After a year with the campaign, I decided to bow out.

I encourage you to look at the place, if any, that alcohol occupies in your home and what impact it can have or is having on your family. After our children were born, Greg and I made the decision to stop serving alcohol at family functions. We seem to have more fun, everyone gets to bed earlier, and we don't have to worry about designated drivers. For our family, it's the right approach. Figure out what works for you.

The issue of drugs is complex. Of course there's a place for pharmacology: pain medications, sleep medications, heart medications, antidepressants, and much more. Use of these must be carefully monitored, however, and decisions must be made about whether they should be a short-term solution or a life plan with medical supervision. I fear some busy doctors today are quick to reach for a prescription pad but are not always focused on steering their patients toward the root causes of their difficulty. Nearly every pill has a side effect—on TV commercials, they're usually glossed over in the final few seconds of a minute-long ad. Contrary to what those commercials seem to imply, prescription drugs, even when obtained from your doctor, are not necessarily the pathway to a perfect life.

So-called recreational drugs can be even more dangerous. Thanks to their increased availability via the Internet, our children are facing risks and choices we parents never had to deal with in our childhoods. Make sure your kids understand that your home is a drug-free zone. Talk to them about what's going on. Many parents hesitate to discuss topics such as drugs, sex, or suicide with their kids because they don't want to introduce them to new and dangerous ideas. But your kids know more than you think they do. It's better that they get straight information from you than potentially distorted and harmful views from a friend or classmate. If your children believe you're open to an honest discussion, they're also more likely to come to you with questions and problems.

Never ignore potential signs of abuse, such as sudden changes in appetite, energy, or personality. If you have suspicions, don't feel that you're violating your child's privacy by insisting on drug testing. Part of establishing a healthy home is playing the role of a parent rather than trying to be your son or daughter's best buddy. We'll talk more about preventing drug abuse in the next chapter.

Having an Emotionally Healthy Home

So far we've focused entirely on matters that relate to good physical health; but equally important to you and your family is developing an environment that promotes strong emotional health. There are many ways to build an emotionally healthy home, but one of the best places to start is with effective communication. Please notice that I said *effective* communication. We all communicate, yet often our words and attitudes don't contribute to positive emotional health. If most statements from one or more family members are met with put-downs, sarcasm, and other belittling comments, that's emotional abuse, and it's far from the healthy home environment that we all desire and need. On the other hand, when you, your husband, and your children can talk with and listen to one another in ways that convey respect and appreciation, you're living in an atmosphere that feels comfortable and loving.

Your family interactions will be most effective if everyone strives to meet three goals: communicate clearly, communicate directly, and communicate with love. Here's one example of how this can work: As moms, we get so busy and work so hard that we don't understand it when our husbands can't see how worn out and frustrated we are. If he isn't able to guess that something's wrong, we may get upset and lash out verbally with words that hurt more than help. It would be better to simply ask for the support we need. Don't drop hints, don't send the message through someone else, and don't wrap it in a layer of anger. Instead, tell your husband clearly, directly, and with love what you need. He'll be grateful that you approached him this way instead of with a personal attack or by giving him the silent treatment. Often, your husband wants to help but just doesn't know what to do.

Even when you and your family are using good communication techniques, you'll still have disagreements. Those differences are an expression of your unique personalities. How you resolve your disagreements, however, will go a long way toward determining the emotional health in your home. Fighting in front of the children, for instance, is never a good idea. Before we had kids, Greg and I had much more colorful disagreements! Now, if there's a conflict between us, we try to "disagree agreeably." If necessary, we'll take our discussion into another room and close the door. Kids are masters at dividing their parents, so even when we're not in complete agreement, we work hard to present unity.

Conflicts between children, meanwhile, have to be handled according to their level of maturity. A three-minute time-out may be just right for a three-year-old (for young kids, I recommend one minute of time-out for each year of life), but a sixteen-minute time-out won't have much effect on a teenager. One great concept developed by psychologists and used in schools for kids in their teen years (and sold by one of our business partners) is called a "peace rug." When two children are in conflict over an issue, you place them on the peace rug. They must share that unified space until they talk through their disagreement and come to a resolution.

Our world would be a healthier place if we adults, particularly husbands and wives, used peace rugs, too. It's important to resolve conflicts quickly so they don't bubble over into bitterness. Fight fair—don't bring up past mistakes or unrelated issues. Remember to look at the issue from your spouse's point of view. And do everything you can to keep your bedroom from becoming a battle zone. The bedroom should be a space for renewal and intimacy. We've all known those nights when, for a time, because of a conflict with your spouse earlier in the day, you experience a period of isolation. But going to bed angry is never a healthy choice for your marriage. Try to resolve any conflicts before you climb into bed.

The principle of learning to share a space—or a toy, a room, or anything else—is one of the most important lessons we can pass on to our children, and definitely one of the keys to a healthy home. Model it for them in your own interactions, and step in when needed to demonstrate sharing compromises that will allow both sides to feel they're being treated fairly. Good sharing skills will frequently end a conflict almost before it starts.

If you can teach your kids how to communicate effectively, resolve conflicts, and share with each other from their earliest days, they'll carry those abilities all the way into adulthood. These skills are the building blocks that will allow each of you to enjoy an emotionally healthy home today and in the years ahead.

Real Solutions

PROBLEM: I know I could use more exercise, but I'm especially concerned about my children. They aren't involved in any school sports and spend far too much time parked in front of the TV or computer. How do I get them moving?

SOLUTION: Plan a family outing.

If you find yourself living with a family of couch potatoes, it may be up to you to uproot them. Make family outings a priority in your schedule. Plan them well in advance so no one is surprised, and expect a few complaints at first.

As parents it's important that we be aware of and set boundaries on our children's activities. Technology—video games, computers, television, iPods—has benefits and the potential for learning. It can also be addictive. Take control and designate times when all these things are turned off and your family gets moving. Once you all get used to being outdoors together, you're likely to find your energetic excursions not only healthy but also a welcome change of pace and an opportunity to draw closer together. Here are just a few ideas:

- Hiking is a classic and affordable recreational activity you can enjoy almost from the time your babies are born. Hiking with children may present a few additional challenges, but it's well worth the effort. Start slowly if you have young children. Try to keep your hikes short, no more than an hour to begin with, and choose trails that offer several exit points so you can stop when your kids show signs of fatigue. Remember to bring sunscreen, bottled water, and snacks such as granola bars, nuts, and fruit.

Be aware of your surroundings. Poison oak is a danger, so keep children on the path. Wash everyone's clothes immediately upon return, and give everyone a good bath, including dogs! I use house-cleaning gloves to wash our dogs, in case they have run through poison oak. I've learned the hard way, and it isn't pretty!

If you aren't near a mountain or forest, consider a park that offers a scenic walking trail. Even if you live in an area where trail hiking isn't an option, walking certainly is. Prepare as if you're headed for the big woods; your kids will enjoy the experience if you make it an adventure.

- Camping is a great way to spend quality time with your family that also provides many opportunities for physical activity. You might lead your kids on a nature hike, or swim or paddle on the lake in a canoe or rowboat. Some large campgrounds include play structures for kids or offer outdoor family games. Even pitching a tent or gathering or chopping firewood can be fun ways to burn calories with your children. If that feels too ambitious, why not set up a tent in your backyard? Just be sure to play some active games to get everyone's hearts pumping.

- Bicycling, if your kids are old enough, is another enjoyable way to encourage fitness and togetherness.

Your destination might be a neighbor's house, the mall, or a movie, depending on your kids' ages and your town's geography. The next time you head out the door with your son or daughter, ask yourself if you can make time to do both of you a favor and leave the car at home. If you have a wide age span in your family, your local college or high school track can be a helpful option. Older kids can ride their bikes around the track (they'll stay in your line of vision even if they're racers), and you can push your little ones in a jogging stroller or carry them in a front pack as you take a brisk walk.

• Skiing, cross-country skiing, and snowshoeing are great winter activities guaranteed to increase your heart rate. Rollerblading is wonderful exercise if you have the means and coordination to try it. Basketball, roller-skating, and ice-skating can be excellent indoor choices if the weather's bad. Swimming can be enjoyed year-round. If you look, you'll find many more options. Try what feels right for your family, and give everyone a few chances to get the hang of it. You'll love what family outings combined with exercise will do for your bodies and for connecting parent and child, brother and sister, and husband and wife.

PROBLEM: I'm a mother in my early forties, and I've heard horror stories about menopause. I'm dreading the day it starts. How can I make this season of my life easier?

SOLUTION: Begin preparing now.

Working on this book has forced me out of denial. As a mom, if you gave birth rather than adopted, you may remember the roller coaster of emotions that your hormones unleashed after your baby arrived. Tears, anxiety . . . coping skills gone out the window. No, you weren't crazy. Biology was just doing its thing.

Menopause is another season of life where biology brings change. Don't be afraid. You're going to get through it. Just be aware that hormones tend to intensify your reality. Examine what's going on and why. Find a doctor who will listen to your concerns, and reject any health care provider who doesn't. Be cautious and careful about any medications that are suggested to you. Be an informed consumer: do your homework and research; don't just watch commercials. If you are going to take any medication go online or to your library after talking with your doctor, your family, and your pharmacist. Know the benefits, side effects, and risks.

This can be a challenging time for any woman. Menopause usually begins between the ages of forty-five and fifty-five and lasts for an indeterminate number of years. Symptoms can include hot flashes; flushed skin; night sweats; insomnia; mood swings marked by irritability, depression, and anxiety; bone density issues; increased risk of heart disease; irregular menstrual periods; spotting of blood in between periods; vaginal dryness and painful sexual intercourse; decreased sex drive; vaginal infections; and urinary tract infections. Not a lot of fun!

You can take steps, however, to reduce the discomfort as your body changes. Regular exercise is highly beneficial. So is a low-fat diet, which should include plenty of calcium and vitamin D. Avoid smoking, which can cause menopause to start early. It's also wise to keep your blood pressure, cholesterol, and other heart risk factors at appropriate levels.[2]

Menopause is a natural event that every woman will experience, but it doesn't have to be something we dread if we take action now. Talk with your doctor about it. Knowledge and preparation are the tools you need to make the smoothest possible transition into the next phase of your life. I'm getting ready now.

PROBLEM: I struggle with rejection. Whenever my husband or children make a negative comment about me, I get defensive. How can I stop taking their words so personally?

SOLUTION: Let rejection help you to grow.

One of the blessings of my modeling career was that it taught me how to deal with rejection. I had plenty of practice! This was a typical day in my life at that time:

- 8 a.m.: race to the subway for a job interview; the photographer at the interview tells me, "Sorry, you're too fat."

- 10 a.m.: another interview and photographer, and again, "too fat."

- Noon: at an interview for a runway job, I'm told, "Kathy, you're too clumsy, and your hair is a poofy bird's nest—do something about it!"

- 1 p.m.: another interview—"too tall."

- 2 p.m.: another interview—"too short."

- 4 p.m.: finally, a real job—until the photographer says, "Kathy, what's that on your forehead? It's a pimple! Look out, everybody, Mount Vesuvius is about to erupt all over our beautiful clothes!"

Later, when our team at Kathy Ireland Worldwide started our business and people told us we were crazy, it really didn't rock my world. I was used to rejection. It still hurt at times, but I knew how to keep it in perspective. Sometimes I even learned from it.

I understand that you may feel rejected right now. It might be your husband or children who are rejecting you in some way. It might be a friend or someone at work. Maybe a rejection from your childhood is still bringing you pain. Whatever the source, I encourage you to treat that rejection as an opinion only. It's one person's viewpoint. You can even tell that person, "Thank you." It doesn't mean you agree with what he or she said. It's simply acknowledging that the person took the time to tell you his or her thoughts.

Please don't let a negative opinion destroy you. As difficult as it can be, you can turn it into a positive. No matter how poorly the message is communicated, be open to hearing what the person is saying. Ask yourself: Is there any bit of truth to this? Do I need to change my attitude or behavior? If so, make a change. Rejection can help us grow if we know what to do with it.

If you decide that what you're hearing is true, don't make excuses. Dame Elizabeth Taylor, a woman I'm mentored by and love dearly, frequently says, "Excuses are so undignified, and they don't absolve you, anyway." A rejection may not be fair. We all need to get over the idea that life is going to be fair. Was it fair for Jesus to take on the sins of the world? All through Old Testament times, people rejected God and worshiped idols. When Jesus came to earth in human flesh, He was hated, mocked, beaten, and brutally murdered. During His most difficult hour, His disciples, who had spent the previous three years experiencing His miracles and love, abandoned Him. When things got scary, they bailed. Peter even denied knowing Him. Our Lord knows all about unfairness and rejection. He understands what you're going through. As difficult as it is, don't let someone else's opinion of you turn into bitterness, resentment, and anger that defeat and define you. You don't want to be a bitter brand.

You are your own brand. You might be thinking, *The girl's gone crazy. I'm not a brand. I'm a person.* Yes, you are a brand. We all are, whether we like it or not. Every encounter we have with someone leaves a lasting brand impression. The question is, what kind of brand are we? Are we kind, loyal, innovative, efficient? Do we get results? Do we consider showing up for work or an appointment ten minutes early as being on time? Or are we perpetually late? Are we negative? Do we have trouble getting along with others? Are we complicated? Do we bring our "personal stuff" with us wherever we go? If we need to make a change, let's do so today.

PROBLEM: My twelve-year-old daughter is losing weight, and I can't understand why. I'm worried that she may be anorexic. How can I tell?

SOLUTION: Watch for the signs, and don't wait to act.

Unexplained weight loss certainly is one of the signs of anorexia and its twin disorder, bulimia. The anorexic either reduces her food intake dramatically or eats a normal meal and then vomits. The bulimic does just the opposite. She binges during meals and then purges by vomiting or using laxatives or enemas. Either disorder can be hidden for some time before anyone notices. Both are terribly dangerous—an anorexic or bulimic can literally starve herself to death if left untreated.

In addition to the behaviors mentioned above, signs that might indicate either anorexia or bulimia include: excessive exercise; dressing in baggy clothes or layers to disguise body shape; obsessing over weight and calorie counts; frequent trips to the bathroom immediately after meals (may include water running in the bathroom to hide the sound of vomiting); use, often hidden, of diet pills, laxatives, ipecac syrup, or enemas; fear of eating meals with others; and low self-esteem.

This is a problem that isn't going away. Today's young people are bombarded with media messages that stress thin bodies, often to an unhealthy degree. Peer pressure also contributes to the perception that girls, especially, must alter their natural body shape to fit in. It's not as common, but boys suffer from anorexia, too. If you suspect that your adolescent is suffering from one of these disorders, don't hesitate—talk to your doctor about it, learn everything you can, and get him or her the help needed.

***

PROBLEM: I have a nine-year-old daughter who's developing a bad habit—she doesn't always tell the truth. How can we communicate when I'm not sure I trust what she's saying?

SOLUTION: Insist on integrity.

There's a phrase that makes me crazy. It's called "a little white lie." Think about that, and I'm sure you'll agree there's no such thing. What is its opposite, a big black lie? Let's not color our lies. Make it clear to your children that the line between honesty and dishonesty is a boundary they don't want to cross, and spell out what will happen if they do. Integrity is the foundation of effective communication, not only within your family but in every interaction in life. If your kids believe it's no big deal to pass on a few untruths now, it will be far too easy for them to fall into a consistent pattern of lies later. Lying is a character flaw that is guaranteed to bring trouble and pain.

Your own behavior in this area, of course, will have a huge influence on your children. If you tell a friend on the phone that you can't join her for shopping that night because of a meeting, and then you spend your evening watching television, what message does that send your child? It's more than just, "Okay, Mom doesn't always tell the truth." It's also, "I guess they won't mind if I make things up, too." It's pretty tough to demand integrity from your kids if you're not living a life of integrity yourself. And lying to your kids is a mistake in judgment that may never be forgotten. Trust takes a long time to earn and yet can be lost in an instant.

Honesty is one key to effective communication, but there are many others. Here are a few more tips that may help your family:

- We moms are in a great position to set the tone in our homes. When your son or daughter makes a statement that you don't agree with, or reacts to you in a snippy manner, make a conscious decision to not "return fire." I'm not suggesting that you excuse rude behavior. Usually, however, by avoiding shouting matches and arguments, you can avoid escalating a situation. For all manner of possible reasons, your child may be upset and need your support. It's best to calmly and firmly remind your son or daughter that your family doesn't tolerate disrespectful language, and then try a loving approach to get to the root of the problem.

  One of our children once saw a school principal intervene in a situation where two classmates had been teasing and harassing another child. Our child said that the principal did a great job of handling it. When I asked how, I learned that the principal didn't get upset; she kept her emotions out of the conversation. She calmly explained why the harassers' behavior was a problem, what the immediate consequences were, what the consequences would be if the behavior continued, and now she was saddened that they had made poor choices. In other words, she set a respectful tone and communicated clearly, directly, and with love. She created an opportunity for forgiveness and growth.

- When you're talking with your family, your body language will communicate just as much (if not more) than your words. If your daughter is starting to open up about the teacher she struggles with at school, show your interest by making eye contact, nodding occasionally, and keeping your arms and legs uncrossed. It might not sound like much, but nonverbal communication reveals a great deal about your attitude, and kids are perceptive. If you're looking around the room, tapping your fingers, or sitting there with a frown on your face and your arms crossed, your child will quickly get the message that you're not interested in her problems.

- Another way to promote effective communication is through family meetings. This is something I learned as a kid from watching the *The Brady Bunch*. Especially when a big change is looming, whether it's the arrival of a baby or a move cross-country, it's important to openly discuss the situation and what adjustments everyone will need to make. After you explain what's coming, invite each member of the family to comment. Listen to your kids' suggestions, and implement them when possible to show that you value their opinions and participation. Try to avoid negative surprises as often as possible. Your children will adapt to change much more readily if they have time to mentally prepare for it.

• When I meet young people who are obviously happy and positive about their lives, I often ask their parents about it. "What are you doing that's working so well? What's your secret?" Usually the answer is something like this: "Our kids always know that we're on the same team. When we're struggling as parents or as a couple, we don't bad-mouth each other in front of them, and we don't draw out issues they don't need to be concerned about. And we never say, 'I'm going to leave you if things don't change.'"

Today's kids live in a complicated world. They don't need the added burden of worrying about their parents' problems or whether their family is going to come apart. If your interactions with your spouse and children contribute to a positive, peaceful, and stable environment at home, then your kids will enjoy excellent emotional health. They will thrive, and so will you.

PROBLEM: My six-year-old is so talkative and inquisitive that I can hardly get a word in. He's always asking me why this and why that. Is it a good idea to keep letting him pepper me with questions?

SOLUTION: Encourage your child's questions.

"Why, Mommy? Why?" It is the oft-repeated question that can drive parents crazy—but I love hearing it! I want our children to be curious. Curious people are never bored or boring. I want our kids to feel comfortable enough to ask me questions about anything.

Of course, it's important to teach respect for others even as we encourage inquisitiveness. Your kids may sometimes need a gentle reminder to listen when others are speaking. But don't discourage the natural inquisitiveness that every child has. A healthy home is one that allows for open dialogue and explanations, not secrecy. Kids who develop the habit of consistently exploring the world around them through questions will grow up to be tomorrow's leaders and peacemakers.

I recently had the privilege of working with an amazing group of women from Gee's Bend, Alabama. Their beautifully designed quilts have been featured on a national tour and now hang in museums across the country and throughout the world. One of these special ladies, Nettie Young, told our children about marching with the Rev. Martin Luther King, Jr. during the civil rights movement. When our kids learned that black and white people used separate drinking fountains, their jaws dropped in collective amazement. Chloe, who was barely two, looked shocked. "Why?" Lily asked, her eyes filled with hurt. And Erik's anger was apparent. Why, indeed. If more people asked questions about what we do and why we do it, that action would help prevent many of the injustices in the world. That three-letter word *why* is the key to unlocking unlimited possibilities.

PROBLEM: My oldest boy is fifteen. He argues constantly with his brother, who's five years younger, and also clashes with his dad. They're all driving me crazy!

SOLUTION: Encourage personal responsibility.

When children of different ages frustrate each other (and Mom), that can be difficult to manage. A common issue is equality. You'll hear comments like "This isn't fair, I did more cleaning than he did!" or "I worked harder than he did!" In those situations, it's important to emphasize that each person is responsible for himself or herself. I tell our children, "You worry about you. Don't worry about the other person. That's not your job."

While you're admonishing your kids, remember to take a good look in the mirror. I've caught myself more than a few times comparing something I'm dealing with to someone else's situation and thinking, *This isn't fair.* Those are the times I need to remember to take my own advice.

To help prevent continual conflicts, share exactly what your expectations are for each of your children, both in terms of home projects and their need to relate to each other. Then make sure that the consequences for meeting or not meeting those expectations are clearly understood and consistently enforced. Remind your children that your expectations will be different for each of them, depending on their age.

Occasionally you may simply need to separate your kids. A little alone time is often the best solution of all.

It's also common for kids moving into their teens to test parents more often as they assert their independence. Older boys often conflict with their fathers and older girls with their mothers as they establish their own identities. The conflict may stem from a desire to assert their independence and be different from Mom or Dad. No matter how much love and respect you have in your home, get ready for conflict.

If you live in a two-parent household, one spouse can play a role in reducing the tension between the other spouse and the child. If your child is battling with your husband and both are frustrated, find times to gently remind your child that your husband loves him or her very much and that his decisions are based on trying to do what's best. Likewise, you may need to remind your husband that the transitional teen years are among the most difficult of a person's life and that your children still need their father's support, whether they act like it or not. Your efforts as mediator can defuse a volatile situation and bring a healthy sense of peace and order to your home.

CHEF ANDRÉ CARTHEN OF ACAFE
Healthy Eating on the Go

As a busy dad myself, I know how hard it can be for parents to fit everything in and provide healthy meals for their family. But you can do it! I encourage you to write down a few favorite recipes that you can turn to when time is short, that are good for you, and that everyone will enjoy. Feel free to make use of the local deli, which has become every mom's best friend. You might purchase some olives, feta cheese, fresh basil, and tomatoes, then mix these at home with pasta, for a wonderful Mediterranean pasta salad. Consider other easy options, such as a rotisserie chicken (remember to remove the fattening skin) with a salad. Or you might put together a great chicken salad in a bed of baby greens; or chop up some chicken, add cucumber and tomato, and place it all in pita bread. Your family will appreciate your healthy choices as well as the taste.

For many parents, trying to get everyone ready for school in the morning is hard enough without trying to plan, prepare, and pack a tasty and nutritious lunch. Here are a few ideas to keep your kids happy and healthy during school days:

- Vary your sandwich breads: fresh rolls, buns, bagels, focaccia bread, pita bread, cornbread, and tortillas are all great options.

- Low-fat choices (chicken, turkey, fish) should top your meat preferences, but don't hesitate to rely on the old standard, peanut butter and jelly. (Did you know that peanut butter contains thirty essential nutrients and phytonutrients?)

- Complement your sandwich with a packaged item such as string cheese, fruit cup, veggie pack, 100 percent fruit or vegetable fruit box, instant oatmeal cup, or fruit and cottage cheese pack.

- When you want to add a sweet taste, choose from graham crackers, yogurt with fruit, dried fruit, trail mix, granola, whole-grain cereal, yogurt-covered raisins, and yogurt-covered pretzels or fruit bars. It's that easy!

Most of us who are raising young children know that often they're very specific about their likes and dislikes. Some don't want different foods to touch each other on their plate. Using plates with dividers can help solve this problem. Left to themselves, our children might never venture to try new foods. Yet it can be fun to introduce our kids to new and even exotic tastes. You might be surprised—they just might discover they have an appetite for a wonderful gourmet meal. Don't be discouraged if this doesn't happen right away. Typically, children need to be exposed to new flavors many times before they acquire a taste for them.

Finally, here are two recipes for healthy, delicious meals that take less than thirty minutes to prepare and will amaze your family and friends. (You can find many more on Kathy's Web site at www.kathyireland.com. Just look for the ACafe logo.) Enjoy!

Balsamic Pepper Seared Pork Chops

4 (4 oz.) boneless, center-cut pork loin chops
1 teaspoon cracked black pepper
salt to taste
cooking spray
½ cup balsamic vinegar
¼ cup chicken broth

Sprinkle both sides of the pork chops with pepper and salt. Coat a medium-size pan with cooking spray, place over medium heat, add pork, and cook on each side for five minutes. When pork chops are cooked, remove from the pan. Deglaze the pan with the chicken broth and balsamic vinegar. Allow to boil for about eight minutes or until slightly thickened, then spoon over chops.

By adding some of your favorite (store-bought) herb potato salad, garnished with a little diced red/yellow bell peppers and a few bits of diced green onion, you will have a light summer meal that serves four people.

Creamy Chicken Spinach Chowder

1 (14.5 oz.) container of chicken stock
2 cans reduced-fat cream of chicken and dumpling soup
1 (10 oz.) package frozen chopped spinach
1 (9 oz.) package grilled chicken strips cut into cubes

Place all ingredients in a pot, bring to a simmer, and serve. This is a great way of turning simple fare into a great family dinner. Serves four people.

Healthy Solutions Checklist

☐ Do you know the status of each family member's fitness and heart health?

☐ Are you familiar with and are you following the revised USDA food pyramid?

☐ Have you developed the habit of eating in moderation?

☐ How often do you and your family exercise?

☐ Are you stretching and working to tone both your upper and lower body?

☐ Are you keeping up with doctor appointments and checking regularly for common diseases and cancers?

☐ Do you maintain a drug-free home?

☐ How effective is your family at communicating?

☐ Are you able to resolve conflicts quickly and peacefully?

☐ Are you passing on good sharing skills to your children?

chapter four

Safe at Home

It seems like I read every day about a child

who is injured or killed in an accident. I

desperately want my home to be a safe haven

for my kids, but where do I start?

*W*hen I think about our three precious children and how much they mean to my husband and me, I can't imagine life without them. Erik, Lily, and Chloe are blessings entrusted to us by God, and we are committed to doing anything and everything we can to protect them from harm. I'm sure you feel the same way about your children—virtually every mom does. Yet despite parents' good intentions, more than 5,000 kids ages fourteen and under die in America each year due to accidents. Injury is the number one killer of our children, taking more lives than disease, violence, or suicide.[1] In every case the story behind the statistic is a heartbreaking family tragedy that could have been prevented. Even the most dedicated parents will miss implementing important safety measures that can make the difference between life and tragic loss. In this chapter I want to talk about how to keep our families from becoming another statistic.

Vehicle Safety

Do you know the most common cause of injury-related deaths of children? If you said "car accident," you're right. In 2005, 1,451 children were killed in automobile accidents in the United States, and more than 200,000 were injured. Nearly half of the children killed in those accidents were not properly restrained in a safety seat or belt.[2]

When you're driving to the grocery store and your baby is screaming or your toddler is squirming, it's tempting to unlatch the safety seat so you can hold him or allow her to stretch. *It's just a short trip*, you may think. *I won't even be on the freeway.* I remember having similar feelings shortly after one of our children was born. My husband and I were leaving a restaurant, and our baby was sleeping. I hated to wake our little one to use the car seat. I just wanted to sit in the passenger seat and tightly hold our baby for the brief drive home. My heart told me it would be safe. Then I remembered the terrible things Greg sees during his shifts in the emergency room. I realized that a seemingly safe situation can change in an instant. At that moment I made the decision that I would not sacrifice our children's safety for anything, including their comfort or sleep.

Even a minor car crash can be a violent event. An unrestrained passenger can be thrown with a force several times his or her weight. Crash forces can cause internal organs to shift, leading to significant injuries. Safety seats and belts are designed, when properly used, to minimize a passenger's motion in a crash, preventing ejection, distributing crash forces over the strongest parts of the body, and protecting the head and spinal cord. It is crucial that children use safety seats and belts and that you check to make sure they're appropriate for your children's size and weight and are in good working condition. While you're at it, check your own safety belts, and remember to wear them each time you drive or ride in a vehicle. I know of a family who secured their baby in a car seat, while the adults riding in the vehicle did not. When an accident occurred, one of the adults slammed into the baby, breaking her ribs and other bones.

When you drive, it's also essential that you keep your attention on the road. Many states are enacting or examining legislation that bans the use of cell phones by drivers. Any potential distraction, whether it's a cell phone, a CD player, or a fast-food meal, has to be carefully considered. Don't endanger yourself or your children for the sake of convenience.

Motor vehicles are also dangerous when your kids are pedestrians or are riding a bicycle. Instruct your children on the rules of the road, and remind them always to be aware of traffic. Hundreds of children are killed each year as they attempt to cross a street or when they dash through a parking lot or run after a ball or toy. Do more than repeat the admonition to look both ways: supervise your young children at all times when they're near any place a vehicle might travel. When your kids are older, make sure they understand the danger and know exactly how to behave when attempting to cross a street. If they're going out at night, insist that they carry flashlights and wear light-colored, reflective clothing. Make sure that all of your family's bicycles are equipped with light reflectors.

Water Safety

Just as supervision is vital to keeping your family safe around motor vehicles, it's also critical any time that your kids are in or near water. Let's say you're filling a tub with water in order to bathe your toddler, or you're relaxing with her beside an outdoor pool. Your cell phone rings. In the ten seconds it takes you to dig the phone out of your purse, your child can fall into the tub or pool. In the two minutes it takes to complete a brief phone conversation, your child can lose consciousness. In the five minutes it takes to make a follow-up call, your child in the tub or pool can sustain permanent brain damage. The most common scenario for a childhood drowning is that someone is supervising a child in or near water but leaves him or her unattended for a brief time. Never ever turn your attention away, even for a moment, from a child who is around water.

Here are a few more water safety tips to remember:

- When your children are swimming in a pool or lake, designate a trusted adult to be the "water watcher"—a person whose sole responsibility is to observe your child and who won't be involved in distractions such as talking on the phone, eating, or reading.

- A responsible adult who is an excellent swimmer must be within arm's reach, at all times, of kids who can't swim.

- If you have small children and own a pool or spa, make sure it has four-sided isolation fencing at least five feet high and is equipped with self-closing and self-latching gates. Install additional barriers of protection, such as pool alarms, pool covers, door alarms, and locks.

- Empty and invert wading pools and buckets immediately after use. A child can drown in just one inch of water.

- When your children are participating in water sports, insist that they wear appropriately sized, Coast Guard–approved personal flotation devices (life jackets). Don't allow air-filled swimming aids, such as "water wings," to substitute for a life jacket.

- Enroll your children by the age of eight in swimming lessons taught by a certified instructor, and teach them the rules of water safety.

Fire Safety

Fire is another heartbreakingly common killer, taking the lives of hundreds of girls and boys each year. You can cut the chances of dying in a home fire in half by installing smoke alarms in each bedroom and on each level of your home and by regularly checking their condition. Recent tests have shown that many sleeping children respond more quickly to an alarm with a message recorded by their parents than to one with a simple tone, however earsplitting it might seem to adults. Watch for these new voice alarms, and decide if they're a better option for your family.

Keep matches, lighters, portable heaters, candles, and other heat sources out of the reach of young children. Make sure candles are at least three feet away from anything that can burn, and place them where they can't be knocked down or blown over. Talk to your kids about what to expect if there is a fire, and plan and practice a fire escape route with your family. Home cooking equipment is the leading cause of residential fires and fire-related injuries, so read the instructions that come with your kitchenware, and be sure you're cooking properly and safely.

Remember to apply fire safety principles to the outside of your home as well. It's wise, particularly if you live in a dry region that's prone to wildfires, to remove anything within thirty feet of your home that might burn easily. This includes plants that contain flammable resins, oils, and waxes. I've had the opportunity to work with the federal Firewise Communities program, which offers many more valuable tips on protecting your home from wildfire. You'll find this information on their Web site at www.firewise.org.

Suffocation

The last of the most common causes of accidental childhood death, especially for kids age six and under, is suffocation. If you're expecting a new baby in your home, buy a crib that meets current national safety standards. The mattress should fit securely in the crib (no more than two fingers of space between crib and mattress) and be free of all plastic wrappings. Remove all soft bedding, toys, and pillows from the crib when your baby is sleeping, and place your baby on his or her back to sleep.

If you have a baby or young children, be sure to immediately put away or throw away the balloons and plastic bags that often are part of children's parties.

Always lock window blinds, whether they're up or down. Make sure your blinds have an attachment on the pull cord so the inner cords can't form a loop that could tighten around your child's neck (blinds sold after November 2000 should have these attachments).[3] Recently, a friend of mine with a toddler was enjoying a moment of quiet in her kitchen when she suddenly realized that it was *too* quiet. She ran to her son's room and found him on top of a stool with a window cord wrapped around his neck. He was okay, but we all thank God she was quick to investigate.

You won't be able to anticipate every threat that your children will encounter during their lives, and I certainly don't advocate keeping your kids in a bubble or worrying needlessly about unlikely dangers. Still, taking preventive steps now will make your home a much safer place to live—and will provide you and your family with much-needed peace of mind.

Managing Messages

As your kids grow older, they will face new hazards beyond the realm of physical injury. They'll contend with issues that kids of previous generations either rarely encountered or never dreamed of: exposure to violence, pornography, and explicit language in media and music; an overtly sexualized society; Internet predators and cyberbullies; and easy access to alcohol and illicit drugs.

On television, in magazines, in movies, in music, in video games, on the Internet, and even on highway signs, the average child is bombarded with hundreds of messages each day that encourage him or her to move in a direction that most parents would not approve. It might be a billboard that promotes gambling or a movie that portrays violence as the solution to every problem. It might be a TV ad that implies they'll fit in only if they wear the "right" jeans, or that if they drive "this" truck, they'll also end up with the girl in the swimsuit. I regret that a few times during my modeling career, I may have contributed to these messages. Growing up in Santa Barbara, wearing a swimsuit was the most natural thing in the world to me. Today, as an older and wiser mom, there are a few photo shoots I wish I'd passed on. When you know better, you do better.

Many of the media's messages are subtle. For example, someone who is smiling and warm and is outwardly handsome or beautiful is often portrayed as good, important, and trustworthy. A person who frowns or who is physically unattractive may be portrayed as insignificant or someone with bad intentions. In the real world, however, true beauty has nothing to do with appearance, and villains are not as easily identified as the cartoon character who twirls his black mustache. I'm reminded of the classic children's book *The Velveteen Rabbit*, in which the wise Skin Horse says, "By the time you are Real, most of your hair has been loved off, and your eyes drop out and you get loose in the joints and very shabby. But these things don't matter at all, because once you are Real you can't be ugly, except to people who don't understand."[4]

How do we help our children understand? How do we protect them from this onslaught of deceptive, negative messages?

It starts with being proactive. As a mom it's vital that you know what your kids are watching, reading, and playing. Ask yourself: Am I comfortable with this show? Does this movie reflect what our family is about? What hidden messages are my kids learning?

Read reviews of television shows, movies, video games, and music before you watch, rent, or buy to help you decide if you're making a wise choice for your family. Make time to watch, play, and listen with your kids so you know what they're experiencing. Don't be afraid to hit the off button if the content is inappropriate, and set limits on your children's screen time. If what you're watching is mostly acceptable but you have reservations, talk with your kids about your concerns. They may not always agree with your thinking, but if your children understand the reasons you object to certain scenes and language, they're more likely to be wary of such material in the future.

For many families, the greater challenge is monitoring what happens when the kids are at someone else's house. You can control the environment in your own home, but how do you protect your children from harmful messages when they're out of sight? If your child is invited to a friend's home for a play date or sleepover and you don't know the parents well, I recommend setting up a meeting with them. Ask the tough questions: Do you have a gun in your house? What do you allow your children to watch on television? What is your take on the latest hit movies? How do you feel about these song lyrics?

I can hear you already: "Kathy, I'm not comfortable with grilling my neighbors!" I understand that. I don't feel comfortable doing it either. I get some funny looks and reactions, believe me! Yet we need to choose our discomfort. Would you rather suffer through a little uneasiness now, before your child is exposed to a potentially harmful environment, or would you prefer to spend endless days and evenings worrying about what your child is doing, seeing, and hearing—or dealing with the fallout after the damage has been done? My advice is to get over yourself—your comfort level is irrelevant when the issue is your family's safety. No one is in a better position or has more responsibility to act as protector and advocate for kids than their mother and father. It's better to learn all you can as soon as you can about the families of your sons' and daughters' friends. If their parenting values are compatible with yours, you'll all be relieved. If they aren't, and you need to turn down an invitation—and possibly discourage a friendship—you'll probably be thankful in the long run.

That said, I'm not at all suggesting that you should never interact with people who are different from you. Our differences enrich us and challenge us to examine our deeply felt beliefs. Do you know the Bible verse, "Let your light shine before men" (Matthew 5:16)? It would be easier for me to avoid people I'm not comfortable with. Yet I believe that God wants us, as Christians, to try to reflect His love and truth to people who may not know or understand Him. Greg and I enjoy seeing our children have opportunities to interact with people of diverse backgrounds, faiths, and cultures. Our kids already have a strong foundation of beliefs, and that's a great comfort. Yet there are limits to what we allow them to see, hear, and do. Wise parents don't let the media or anyone else subject their children to improper influences.

A Wired World

The World Wide Web has become woven into nearly every aspect of our lives. That's positive in that it has opened up wonderful new avenues for fast and efficient communication and for acquiring knowledge. When our children need to do a school report on the history of Argentina, the information they need can be found in moments. In fact, many schools and teachers now require that their students use the Internet to complete assignments. The flip side of that coin, though, is that kids today are too often exposed to material, people, and pressures that are destructive.

One example of this is pornography. According to at least one survey, more than 40 percent of Web users age ten to seventeen see sexually explicit images online each year, and two-thirds of those run across the images accidentally while surfing the Internet.[5] Those are disturbing numbers when you consider how addicting pornography can be, especially for visually-oriented boys. Early exposure to sexual images can be traumatic for any child.

Then there's cyberbullying, which can involve anything from posting a list of "uncool" kids on a Web site, to spreading rumors by e-mail, to harassing via instant messaging. There are examples, like that of Courtney Katasak of Kennesaw, Georgia. Courtney received an unidentified instant message. When she replied, asking who it was, the sender responded with teasing lines and a link to a porn site. "Then they kept sending me these inappropriate messages," Courtney said. "It freaked me out."[6]

One frightening aspect of the Internet is its ability to mask the identities of users. In a wired world, anyone can send a message and pretend to be someone he or she is not. You may have heard about the sixteen-year-old Michigan girl who tricked her parents into getting her a passport and then flew to the Middle East to see a man she'd met online. U.S. officials there intercepted her before the meeting and persuaded her to return home.

The story of Megan Meier did not end as well. Megan, a thirteen-year-old in Missouri, corresponded with a boy named Josh on an online social networking site for six weeks in 2006. When Josh wrote one day that he didn't want to be Megan's friend anymore, she became terribly upset. Then electronic bulletins appeared with statements such as "Megan Meier is a slut" and "Megan Meier is fat." Josh reportedly wrote that Megan was a bad person and that the world would be better off without her. Megan, who already struggled with depression, was distraught. Her parents tried to reassure her. Twenty minutes later, they discovered that their daughter had hanged herself in her bedroom. Megan died the next day. A few weeks later Megan's parents learned that "Josh" did not exist. He'd been made up by members of a neighboring family.[7]

What can you do to counteract these appalling possibilities? The obvious solution is to take your kids offline, but that may not be practical in today's computer-dependent world. One great step is to keep your Internet-wired computer in a commonly used space, such as a family room, where it's easy to monitor what your kids are doing and viewing. I urge you to keep the Web out of your children's bedrooms—it's an arrangement that is asking for trouble. Wherever your computer or computers are, install filters that help block harmful content (you may want them for yourself as well), but don't rely on them to screen out everything you don't want your kids to see.

Be wary of social networking services, such as MySpace and Facebook, and video sharing services, such as YouTube. Some people have charged that these services provide online predators and sex offenders easy access to unsuspecting children. The book *MySpace®, MyKids* by Jason Illian has been a great resource for me in learning about MySpace and how to talk with our children about online communication. I agree with the author's position that a home is not a democracy. It's a good idea to regularly check your kids' online viewing history. I don't believe in societal censorship. As parents, however, we must supervise what our children see and experience.

It's also important to set limits on how long your kids can be on the computer and what sites they can visit, and to talk with them about what they're doing online. Teach them that respect for others applies just as much online as anywhere else. And again, talk with the parents of your children's friends so you know and agree with their rules for Internet use when your kids are visiting. If you're diligent, you have a much better chance of protecting your children from the dangers that are only a mouse click away. To learn more about Internet safety, visit www.safesurfinusa.org, the Web site for a powerful organization led by my friend Erik Estrada and concerned law enforcement officials and parents.

Predators

We've already mentioned the sad fact that some people look for opportunities to prey on children. You can help prevent the unthinkable by talking with your kids about "stranger danger." Let them know that they should never accept a ride or even approach a car driven by someone they don't know.

The majority of child sexual abuse cases, however, involve someone that the child already knows. It's imperative that we make our children aware, from the earliest age possible, that their bodies belong to them and that no one should touch their private areas or speak to them in ways that seem threatening. We've always taught our kids that if someone makes them feel at risk, even if that person is a family member or someone they've known a long time, then all the rules go out the window. We want them to scream, hit, bite, kick, and run—whatever it takes to get out of that situation.

I know of a boy, about twelve years old, who was approached in a theme park by a woman in a character costume. The costumed employee was extremely friendly. She put her arm around the boy and said, "Wouldn't you love to have a picture with the two of us?" The boy answered, "No, I don't really want to." The woman persisted and did not back off until the boy said in a loud voice, "No, thank you!" The person in the costume may have had the best intentions, but it was wonderful that this child knew how to handle the situation and had the courage to set the boundary.

It's also wise for you and your family to establish a code word that can be used if something unexpected happens and you need a friend to pick up your kids. Tell your children that it's only okay to get in the car if that person knows the code word. Teach your kids about whom to talk to if they ever become separated from you. Gavin de Becker, a leading security expert, does not recommend teaching children to go to the police when lost. To small children, security guards look like police officers. Gavin de Becker's first recommendation for a lost child is to find a mom and ask for help. Consider providing your kids with a bracelet or other means of identification that includes a way to contact you. When children are too young to remember their phone number, I recommend writing it on their skin with a marking pen whenever you're out and could get separated.

Finally, when you meet strangers or new friends or parents of your children, trust your intuition. We may have the finest computer filters and safety systems, but they are only tools—they're not foolproof. I believe that, for mothers especially, intuition is a God-given talent that should not be wasted. When someone is making you uncomfortable, listen to your inner voice. In business we're taught to feel the fear and move forward anyway. That may be a good business strategy, but it's the wrong approach for your family. There's a reason we moms are sometimes compared to a lioness with her cubs. We're both fiercely committed to protecting our young—no matter what.

Healthy Rebellion

We've been talking about ways to keep your family safe by shielding them from outside threats and pressures. Some dangers, though, your kids may step into willingly. In these cases, knowledge may be your best form of protection.

We're all aware of the temptations and risks of premarital sex. Nearly half of American high school students have had sexual intercourse. More than 8 percent of girls age fifteen to nineteen become pregnant. Approximately one out of four sexually active young people contracts a sexually transmitted disease such as human papillomavirus (HPV), trichomoniasis, chlamydia, hepatitis, or HIV/AIDS. The U.S. Centers for Disease Control and Prevention estimates that more than one-third of teenagers are infected with HPV.[8] Even more frightening, we are breeding more resistant strains of some of these diseases and new "superbugs" that are difficult to cure. We are the only species on the planet with the potential to destroy ourselves through the act of mating.

Your kids need to know these facts. Parents must decide when is the right time to talk about sex with their kids, but please don't wait long. It's better to speak too soon than too late. I've had the pleasure of spending time with Dr. Robert Schuller and his family. His daughter Gretchen graciously shared with me a series of books (the Learning About Sex Series by Rich Bimler) on sex education. They're great because they are matter-of-fact, present a Christian point of view, and include a book for each age. I remember feeling embarrassed when I started reading them and thinking about discussing them with our kids. Then I thought, *Wait a minute. If I'm too embarrassed to talk to them, how are they going to talk to me and ask me questions down the road?* I got over my embarrassment and went through the books with our children.

Having "the first talk" is important, but please don't stop there. If you want to establish a safe environment for your children, you must maintain an open dialogue with them. Let them know that when people talk about "safe sex," what that really means is *safer* sex. Yes, condoms are safer than no protection at all. But condoms break. And condoms won't protect anyone from a broken heart. Be clear about letting your kids know where you stand on the issue of premarital sex and why. Talk to them about the emotional impact of sexual intimacy. Once a person gives himself or herself to another person sexually, that can never be taken back. How many young girls—and boys too—have discovered what seems like love and begun a sexual relationship, only to discover that it wasn't love at all? How many have fallen into genuine love, then learned too late that it wasn't the enduring love that leads to lifelong marriage? A true love will always be willing to wait until marriage for sexual intimacy. Challenge your kids to think about a couple of key questions: Could physical intimacy now lead to enormous emotional pain later? Is sex worth the risk to their health and even their lives?

In our family and in millions of others, of course, premarital sex is a moral issue as well as a matter of emotional and physical health. God does not want to keep us or our children from pleasure. He does want to keep us from pain. If we desire to live according to His plan, we must accept that premarital sex is not His choice for us.

An open dialogue is just as important when addressing the issues of alcohol and drug use. I've already shared that our family no longer serves alcohol at social gatherings, and we certainly don't condone the use of drugs. Talk with your kids about the laws and physical and emotional risks associated with alcohol and drug use and abuse. Explain your own feelings. Be on the lookout for any signs of trouble, and consider making it easier for your kids to resist drugs and alcohol by removing temptation.

Even prescription drugs can lead to problems. One of my closest friends, a man who is like a brother to me, has been in recovery from alcohol and drug abuse for twenty-five years. He has talked freely about the fact that he used to check his mother's medicine cabinet for pills. He realized that if he took one or two pills from one bottle and a couple more from another, no one would notice the difference. Recognize that your kids are at an age when experimentation is common. Don't unintentionally encourage them by leaving alcohol or prescription pills around that ought to be removed from your home or locked away.

When you talk about all of this with your children, let them know something else: people who live healthy, empowered lives by making wise choices often find themselves in the minority. Encourage them to accept and draw strength from that. Most kids want to rebel at some point in their lives. Tell them that this is their chance! I rebelled at times against the "in" crowd when I was younger. When I was at a party during my modeling days and someone offered me drugs, I said no. When a photographer asked me early in my modeling career to take off my top, I said I wasn't comfortable doing that. He told me I wouldn't make it in the business if I didn't; when I still refused, he crossed the line and actually pushed me physically. I'm not a violent person, but I had to push him back. I walked off the job.

That photographer was wrong. I didn't have to compromise what I believed in to succeed. Neither will your kids. I remember being in junior high and wanting desperately to fit in and be like everyone else. We all feel that way sometimes. But it's better to be an example for your friends than to blindly follow them. Remind your sons and daughters that instead of trying to fit in, what's most important is being true to yourself and the plan God has for you. That's the approach that will keep them on a safe and healthy path for the rest of their lives.

Real Solutions

PROBLEM: I want to do more to protect my family from potential physical hazards. What measures can I take?

SOLUTION: Act now to prevent emergencies such as falls, poisonings, and firearm injuries.

Three more common and preventable childhood injuries are falls, poisonings, and firearm wounds. Here are some tips on avoiding each.

FALLS

Thousands of children are injured in falls each year, particularly from bunk beds, shopping carts, bleachers, and open windows. One of my mottoes is to hope for the best but plan for the worst. Common sense and a few preventive steps will help keep your family safe:

- Teach your kids that rough play is unsafe around bunk beds and that only one child should be on the top bunk at a time. Don't allow children under age six to use a top bunk. In the emergency room, my husband frequently sees the results of careless horseplay on bunk beds: young kids with broken limbs.

- Securely attach bunk-bed ladders, and use only the appropriate size mattress for the bed. Fasten supports to ledges of bunk beds with screws or bolts.

- Affix to a wall any piece of furniture in your home, such as a bookcase, that could fall and injure a child. The coworker of a friend recently received a tragic phone call at the office. His toddler had climbed up a bookcase, and it had toppled over on him. He was killed. With any large furniture we sell at Kathy Ireland Worldwide, we make available a tip kit for securing it to the wall. If you purchase a large piece that doesn't include a tip kit, go to the hardware store and buy the material you need to make it safe for your young ones.

- Any spaces between bunk-bed guardrails and bed frames should be less than three and a half inches, and guardrails should extend at least five inches above the mattress to keep kids from rolling off.

- Always use a harness or safety belt to restrain children in shopping-cart seats. Don't let your child stand up in or push a shopping cart, and stay close to the cart at all times.

- Closely examine bleachers before your children sit down; many are decades old and in disrepair. Supervise kids closely, and warn them about the danger of falling through spaces under the seats.

- Don't allow children to play near an open window. Remind them that window screens can pop off easily and that even closed windows can break.

POISONINGS

Curiosity is a wonderful trait to see in young children, but it can also lead them into trouble, especially when lethal substances are accessible. Consider the following advice on ways to reduce this threat to your family:

- Know which household products and medications are poisonous, and store them out of sight and reach of your children. Remove poisonous plants.

- Keep all products in original containers, and buy child-resistant packaging.

- Never leave poisonous household products unattended during or after use. A poisoning can occur in seconds.

- Install carbon monoxide detectors in your home.

- Post the national toll-free poison hotline number near every telephone: 1-800-222-1222.

It's also so important for you to be aware of the chemicals in your home and workplace. One of my dear friends lost her daughter to lung cancer. She wonders now if there was a link between the cancer and the chemicals she used as a beautician. We're seeing higher cancer rates today than previous generations did. Think about the potential toxins that surround you. If your home was built before 1978, have it tested for lead-based paint. Consider organic alternatives to the chemicals you use. We're still learning about many of these hazards, so the less your family is exposed to these substances, the better.

FIREARMS

The common factor in every unintentional gun injury is access to a loaded firearm. If you are a parent and a gun owner, the most important steps you can take are to reduce your kids' access to firearms and to safely store all guns.

- Ask yourself if the benefit of keeping a firearm at home is worth the risk to your children.

- Keep firearms unloaded, and keep them and the ammunition locked up. Store them in separate locations and out of the reach of children. Use quality gun locks on every firearm. Keep gun storage keys and lock combinations hidden in a separate location.

- Talk to your children about the dangers of guns. Teach them never to play with a firearm and to tell a trusted adult if they find one.

- Ask the parents of your kids' friends if they have firearms and what safety procedures they follow.[9]

Help! This Is an Emergency!

Every second counts in an emergency. With a little planning, you'll be much better prepared to make efficient use of those valuable first moments when the unexpected happens. One vital step is to prepare an emergency phone numbers list that can be posted near every phone in the house. If you're a cell phone only family, post these lists in several easy-to-find locations. Each list should include phone numbers for ambulance, fire, and police services (911 in most areas); poison control; your children's doctors and dentists; electric, oil, and gas companies; your own home, work, and cell phone numbers; your address; and the phone numbers of legal guardians or other relatives or friends who can be contacted if parents are injured or unreachable. Make a copy of this list for your car and diaper bag.

It's also wise to keep an emergency first-aid book, poison-control kit, fire extinguisher, and flashlights in easily accessed locations in your home. Replace your fire extinguisher every year, keep fresh flashlight batteries on hand, and consider purchasing a flashlight that doesn't depend on batteries. Make sure everyone in the family knows where your emergency items are. Schedule times to learn the Heimlich maneuver and CPR (cardiopulmonary resuscitation) today—don't put it off.

If you are faced with an emergency, start by taking a deep breath and staying calm. If the victim is seriously injured or unresponsive, call 911 immediately. Begin CPR if the victim isn't breathing. If the victim is bleeding, apply continuous pressure to the wound with a clean cloth. When your kids are old enough, talk to them about what to do in an emergency. Make sure that they and your babysitter know your home address and phone number. In an emergency, a 911 operator will ask for this information.

PROBLEM: I've heard about kids buying cough and cold medicine to get high. How do I make sure my children don't try something crazy like that?

SOLUTION: Keep them talking while you're watching.

According to a recent government survey, about 3.1 million people between the ages of twelve and twenty-five have intentionally misused over-the-counter cough and cold medicines, which is more than 5 percent of American teens and young adults.[10] A growing trend among young people is to use ingredients found in over-the-counter medications to make methamphetamine, a highly addictive psychostimulant. In the last few years, growing concern about the abuse of over-the-counter medications has led to state and federal laws that limit the amount of certain medicines that may be purchased within specific time periods. That's a step in the right direction, but it's not enough to put an end to these behaviors.

Another recent and disturbing trend among young people is the abuse of household products, known among users as "whiteout," "sniff," or "huff." A person gets a bag, fills it with cleaning products or substances such as glue, paint, lighter fluid, fingernail polish, permanent markers, deodorant, or correction fluid, and inhales. This can cause brain damage, hearing loss, heart failure, and kidney and liver damage. It can also kill.

A variation of this behavior is called "dusting." I learned of a family that worked hard to stay up-to-date on the drug culture. As far as the parents knew, none of their kids had ever tried drugs. The father brought home a large can of Dust-Off, a product designed to blow compressed air to clear dust and debris from computers. What this family didn't realize was that Dust-Off also contains a propellant that, when inhaled, inhibits oxygen flow to the brain. Two mornings later, when the mother tried to wake up her fourteen-year-old son, she couldn't. The can of Dust-Off he'd inhaled from was still in his hands. He was dead.

There is no foolproof method for keeping your kids away from these or any drugs or substances. Yet by talking regularly with them about the dangers of drug use, as well as about everything else going on in their lives—and by listening closely to their answers—you'll be in a much better position to keep them informed and to provide the support they need when they have problems. Pay attention to the latest trends in so-called recreational drug use; learn all that you can. And watch your kids closely. Be aware of any changes in behavior, and react calmly but swiftly. If you are involved and observant, you'll communicate that your children are important to you and that you care. That's often the best antidrug strategy of all.

PROBLEM: I just learned that a high-school friend of my daughter's has been cutting herself with a knife. Why would someone do this? Is there anything I can do to discourage my kids from doing it?

SOLUTION: Yes—love, honor, and guard your children.

Self-mutilation or self-injury, also known as "cutting," appears to be on the rise in America, particularly among adolescent girls and young women. The roots of this behavior are usually complex but may include low self-esteem and feelings of anger, emotional pain, fear, and hate. Though obviously destructive, it is how some people release overwhelming tension and cope with unmanageable feelings. People who injure themselves usually go to great lengths to hide their wounds and scars; they feel shame even though they keep doing it.

I know of one young woman, Tracy (not her real name), who took a knife and began cutting her shoulders and inner thighs at the age of fourteen. Her father was physically abusive. Her mother had moved out of their home. She felt she had no purpose in life and no future. At age nineteen Tracy had an abortion; the cutting grew worse. Only after she entered a live-in ministry for broken young women did she begin to heal physically and emotionally.[11]

Even though cutting appears to be on the increase, it's hardly new. I was part of a group that traveled to Israel recently and stood on Mount Carmel, the same place where Elijah confronted the prophets of the false god Baal centuries before. Our pastor, who accompanied us on the trip, reminded us that the followers of Baal called on their god for hours, asking him to ignite their sacrifice. When Elijah taunted them, they "shouted louder and slashed themselves with swords and spears, as was their custom, until their blood flowed" (1 Kings 18:28). Their self-destructive behavior made no difference, of course. Only when Elijah called on the true God did flames light up the mountain. This powerful example from the Bible reminded me that evil in all its forms has been around for a very long time.

As our pastor talked with us about Elijah, he shared that a couple of years ago, parents were coming to him with concerns for their children who were cutting themselves. He was deeply distressed about this. After praying, he felt led to this passage of Scripture: "When midday was past, they raved until the time of the offering of the evening sacrifice; but there was no voice, no one answered, and no one paid attention" (1 Kings 18:29 NASB).

Please know that this is a tragedy that can occur in the most loving of homes, where parents are paying attention and where children do receive love. If one of your kids is involved in this terrible practice, don't give up or lose hope. Persevere, and never cease praying for your precious children.

What are some things we can do to try to prevent this from happening? Let your children know how much you love and value them. Encourage them to share their feelings, and remember to honor those feelings even if you disagree with them. Teach your kids appropriate ways to respond to stressful situations; help them to see options for dealing with problems. Avoid any form of physical or emotional abuse in your home. And if you do find out that one of your children is cutting, seek professional help immediately.

PROBLEM: I'm a single mom, and I recently heard about AEA. I want to discourage my boys from trying it, but I just don't know if I can handle that conversation.

SOLUTION: Get past your uneasiness and explain the dangers.

AEA is the acronym for autoerotic asphyxiation, which is the practice of a person reducing oxygen flow to the brain, usually by "controlled" strangulation or suffocation, to enhance feelings of pleasure during masturbation. When a partner is involved, it's called erotic asphyxiation. Obviously, this activity is extremely dangerous. People may use belts, cords, scarves, or ties to produce the effect they seek, or they may put their head in a plastic bag. Many try to rig a rescue mechanism to stop the asphyxiation, but the "failsafe" often fails. Anywhere from a few hundred to several hundred people—most often teenage boys—die in the United States each year attempting erotic or autoerotic asphyxiation. Some people, including parents, experts, and health officials, say the numbers are higher, because they believe that many deaths ruled as suicide may have involved AEA.

A deadly variation of AEA is the "choking game," where kids—especially those who don't have access to drugs—get together and asphyxiate each other to get high. This too can be a fatal pastime.

Some of the signs of erotic asphyxiation or choking include unexplained or dubious explanations for marks or bruises on the throat; headaches; bloodshot eyes and/or redness around the eyes; finding belts or similar items lying around or tied in knots; and frequent locking of bedroom doors.

Many parents are uncomfortable with talking about this disturbing behavior, particularly with their children. I certainly understand that. But my advice, again, is to choose your discomfort. Would you rather have a difficult conversation now or live with the knowledge that your family could one day face a nightmare? Even if you feel there is no chance that your children are considering or practicing this behavior, you still need to make them aware of it. You may not be talking about it, but you can be sure that their friends are. Get past your uneasiness and explain the dangers. You might be saving your child's life.

PROBLEM: Both a male relative and a family friend abused me physically and sexually when I was a child. I am taking steps to deal with my past and am seeing a counselor. How do I know I won't someday abuse my own kids?

SOLUTION: Learn how to break the cycle.

My heart breaks for anyone who has suffered and survived abuse and trauma. I have tremendous admiration for women and men who are actively rejecting the destructive behaviors in their past. Child abuse is a tragedy that often is passed from one generation to the next, but it does not have to continue. If this is historical behavior in your family, you must be the one who breaks the cycle. Learn to use your pain to build a bridge of hope. Cycles continue when we play that "ostrich" game and live in denial. To break a cycle, we need to deal with our pain. That doesn't mean dwell on it, but dealing with it can take time. Don't be hard on yourself. Taking that step to face your past, deal with it, and move on is a good indicator that the abusive cycle will end with you.

I am truly grateful to and have great admiration for all people who have suffered childhood trauma and have found ways to use those terrible experiences for good. One close member of my business family endured a horrific childhood. He witnessed the shooting of a family member and summoned help while the victim was bleeding all over him. He was beaten by his mother on a regular basis. He was victimized sexually by an older sibling. This man used the experience and pain of those tragedies to become one of the most helpful people I know. He chose to break the cycle and become a loving father, uncle, friend, and godparent. He also has strong risk-assessment skills and regularly is involved in security procedures for our team.

No matter what our background, we all have the ability to be warriors for the Lord and to protect young lives. We must choose not only to never practice abuse but also to put an end to it whenever and wherever we can. If you are determined—and if you educate yourself on proven methods for success and trust in God to take care of the rest—you can make a difference. I make sure our children and my husband know that I am on their team—my love for them is unconditional. I may not agree with every choice they make, but there's nothing we can't get through together, and nothing will ever take my love away. I also make sure our kids know that while I pray that their mistakes will not have devastating consequences, some mistakes do not allow for a second chance.

Other damaging behaviors sometimes passed down through the generations are alcohol and drug abuse. If you've struggled with these addictions, I urge you, for the sake of your kids, to seek the help you need. We must give our children every opportunity to be the blessings to the world that God intended them to be. Of course, even some of the most loving families, including those with no history of alcohol or drug addiction, will find themselves dealing with these issues. None of us is immune. Yet your efforts to be a role model for your children do make a difference. The example you set, including persevering through failure, can be the encouragement they need to stay on course toward their destiny.

Safe Solutions Checklist

☐ Do you know the most common causes of childhood death and injury, and are you taking steps to minimize the risks to your family?

☐ How closely do you monitor your children's media activity, particularly their use of the Internet and e-mail?

☐ Are you talking with your kids about the media messages they're receiving?

☐ Have you talked with the parents of your kids' friends about their rules and values?

☐ Do your children know what to do if someone they don't know approaches them?

☐ Do your kids know how to respond if someone tries to touch them inappropriately?

☐ Have you talked with your kids about the risks of premarital sex, alcohol, and drugs? Are the communication lines still open?

☐ Do your kids understand the concept of healthy rebellion?

☐ Do you keep all drugs, household cleaning products, and weapons in safe, inaccessible locations?

☐ Have you posted emergency phone number lists in your home, and are they up to date?

chapter five

Your Best You

I'm so busy and stressed that I don't know

who I am anymore. I just try to get through

each day. I need a plan for my life!

Can you help?

When you were young, did you ever dream about what you wanted to be when you grew up? I know I did. I wanted to be a newspaper reporter because of my thirst for knowledge, a marine biologist because of my love of the ocean, and a teacher because of my love for children. For all of us, those childhood dreams are part of the process of discovering the person we were meant to be. They are first glimpses into our future, when we look beyond who we are into the mist of what we might become. They're early snapshots of what it may mean to be our best.

Do you still remember those childhood dreams? More important, do you still dream? There are so many mothers who began their marriages with the highest hopes for their future. They couldn't wait to start a family. They had goals for the kind of wife and parent they wanted to be. They anticipated watching their individual character and faith develop and looked forward to nurturing the same in their children. They saw themselves involved in exciting careers and causes and making a difference in the world.

Many of these same moms are in a different place now.

They're weighed down by the burdens and distractions of daily life. They're uninspired and depressed. They feel trapped and no longer have a clear vision for their future. They're worried about their children in a world that can be dangerous.

If this describes your life, I'm so glad you picked up this book. Living without your dreams is miserable and unnecessary. Even when we're frustrated, sad, or furious, it's like the cliché about the glass of water. Half empty? Half full? Your decision. If you're not living your dreams, you're missing the many wonderful choices available to you. If you want to become your best you, it's time to rediscover and nurture your dreams. The first step is to honestly explore where you've been, where you are, and where you want to go.

Dreams and Obstacles

Let's ask and answer some tough questions. This will be most effective if you do it when you're not distracted by family or other responsibilities. Please write down your answers on paper or type them into your computer. Give yourself time to reflect, concentrate, and put down what's on your mind and in your heart—no one-word or one-sentence answers allowed. If necessary, ask your husband, a friend, or a family member to watch the kids for a while. If you don't have anyone to help you, this is a rare occasion when I'd recommend letting some approved television or video entertainment keep your kids occupied. Your family, whether you are part of a traditional couple with kids or a single mom, will benefit from your taking this time for yourself. Take more than one session if you can't finish now.

Are you ready? Here we go.

1. What are your dreams for yourself, your marriage, your family, and your career? What do you want each of those areas to look like next month, next year, five and ten years from now?

2. If you're married, what kind of wife do you want to be? If you're single and don't want to stay that way, what kind of husband are you looking for?

3. What kind of mother do you want to be?

4. How do you define *success*?

5. In which of the areas listed above are you succeeding? What are you doing that makes this true?

6. In which of the areas listed above do you feel you're not succeeding? What's blocking you in each of these areas? Be specific.

7. What can you do, starting today, to take away the obstacles, move you closer to your dreams, and achieve success in each of the areas you listed for number six?

If this emotional exercise has brought you to tears because your dreams seem unattainable, your successes are vastly outnumbered by "failures," and you don't know how to remove the obstacles, please don't be discouraged—that's what this book is for! I can't guarantee that we'll solve all of your problems by the final page. I can tell you that the road will not always be easy. My life is far from perfect, but I love seeking and sharing answers. Many of the lessons on these pages have sunk into my thick head only after plenty of those "failures." I promise that we are covering important ground for any mother and wife and that the solutions will help you become your best you—the person you were born to be.

My confidence in your potential isn't based only on experience. I place my faith and life in the hands of God. I was eighteen, insecure, and frightened when I realized that God truly loved me. I made the decision then to trust Him above all others. I believe in a compassionate God who has created each of us for a unique purpose. He does not make mistakes. He has given you the most cherished of gifts, the gift of lives—yours and your children's. He would not bestow that honor and responsibility on you without a wonderful plan for your future.

One of my favorite Bible verses, Jeremiah 29:11, says: " 'I know the plans I have for you,' declares the LORD, 'plans to prosper you and not to harm you, plans to give you hope and a future.'" God wants to give each of us hope and a future. The problem, too often, is that we miss out on that future because we let something get in the way.

Anchors and Engines

Many moms say they are filled with self-doubt. They have little confidence in their abilities as a parent. They may pretend in front of their friends and even their own family that they have it all together, yet on the inside they feel overwhelmed and incapable of managing their lives. Their self-image takes real punches every day. These women think their abilities are a poor match for the commitments and responsibilities they confront each day, and they secretly believe that someone else is doing a much better job. Usually it just isn't true.

If you are one of these moms, I have three questions for you: Who knows your children better than you? Who is in a better position to be the mother they so desperately need? And who else can achieve the purposes that God has designed specifically for you? The answer in each case, of course, is you— and only you. You are uniquely qualified to parent your child. You're also the best-qualified person to fulfill your destiny.

For every job I've ever had, I've been required to go through an application process—with one exception. That exception was becoming a mom, which is the most important position of all. I'm guessing you didn't apply for your job as a mom either, unless you were blessed with the precious gift of adoption. If that is how you became a mom, I want to say a special prayer and thank you. You're amazing. When God established the position of mom for your family, He already had you in mind. He created you specifically for that role. He knows you can do it and is ready to guide you through each step. Your job is to accept the position, trust His judgment, and listen to His direction.

Lena Horne performed a beautiful song, written by Michel Legrand and Hal David, with these lyrics: "Let me be your mirror . . . and you will be beautiful forever." Those lyrics contain a powerful message. If we allow God to be our mirror, we begin to see ourselves as He does rather than how we think others see us or how TV commercials or fashion magazines tell us we should feel about ourselves. True self-esteem comes from understanding our value to God. The Bible says that God created each of us in His own image. That's as good as it gets. When we remember that truth, we can be absolutely certain of our dignity and worth.

How is it, then, that we so often have a distorted image of ourselves? For many of us it stems from the negative messages we hear or whisper to ourselves each day. Maybe someone cruelly said that you were ugly or inept or worthless. That abuse, whether verbal, physical, or both, is damaging. You have to acknowledge that pain in order to let it go and heal. You might have reinforced that negative message by repeating it to yourself over the years. It doesn't take long for that message to turn into a limiting self-belief. When that happens, you're allowing someone else's unhealthy opinion to override God's wisdom and block you from His plan. It's an obstacle you must cast aside to release your potential.

In order to be the parent, spouse, and person you want and were meant to be, you don't have the luxury of allowing negativity in your life. Think about a speedboat on a lake. It's designed to cut through the water at high velocity, leaving impressive ripples in its wake. The powerful engine propelling it makes the journey appear effortless. But what happens when the speedboat's anchor is resting on the bottom of the lake? No matter how much you gun the engine, the boat goes nowhere.

Anchors are useful tools when you want to stay in one place for a while. They can stabilize your boat or your life. Too many of us, however, want and need to move forward but are stuck because we're trying to drag an anchor along behind us. The next time you catch yourself saying or thinking a negative message about yourself, ask: do I want to be an anchor or an engine? Limiting self-beliefs weigh you down. Accepting your God-given value moves you forward. Choose consistently to be an engine, and those false beliefs will begin to fall away.

Family and friends can be engines or anchors too. Seek out people who will encourage you to reach for your dreams. When we started our business with a line of designer socks, John and Marilyn Moretz were our first brand partners. They believed in us and in our vision. Today they are not only cherished partners but also members of our extended family. John and Marilyn gave us our wings and taught us to fly.

If you find that the people around you are holding you back, talk with them about it. Help them see who you really are and what you need from them. If they won't help, you don't have to remove them from your life . . . just put their point of view in perspective. Know where they're coming from, and let them know where you're going. Family relationships can be complex, but your persistence in this area is vital. If your extended family doesn't get it, you may need to find ways to reduce the time you spend with them. If your friends continue to weigh you down with negative comments, it may be time to seek out new "engine" friends who will help you move forward. You can't be stuck unless you choose to be stuck.

Reject that option today. Make a promise to yourself to move forward, and keep it.

Feeling the Fear

Another common obstacle to becoming your best is one we all face regularly: fear. Most surveys indicate that public speaking is the single greatest fear for men and women (death is second!). I can relate to that. I still have anxiety before speaking in public.

I remember the first time I gave a business speech. It was at a Palm Springs, California, hotel where a few years earlier my business team and I had been chased off the property for taking photos (we didn't know we needed a permit). Now I'd been invited back to speak on the topic of business to hundreds of people. In the minutes before I was scheduled to go up to the podium, my hands were sweating and my heart was pounding. I was so nervous that I wanted to crawl under the table and hide. It was pure terror. I mentioned my nervousness to the man sitting next to me, a friend I also consider a member of my family. His response, offered in a loving but powerful tone, wasn't quite what I expected.

"Kathy, you need to get over yourself," he said. "This isn't about you. There are people out there who need your best, who need the information and insights you have to offer. You're in a unique position to share what they want to hear. So go for it!"

He was right. Each of us has gifts and knowledge we need to pass on, whether it's with our family or the world. When we don't, we fall short of our purpose and rob someone else of our best.

What is our fear all about, anyway? We don't want to look foolish in front of others. We don't want to make a mistake. We don't want to fail. At the core, I believe it's a lack of trust in ourselves and the plan God has laid out for us. We're afraid that we aren't good enough, aren't smart enough, or aren't capable, so we hold back. And in the process, we miss out on fulfilling our destiny and being of service to others.

I don't mean to imply that when you trust in yourself and God's plan you should expect the fear to disappear. I try to discern and follow His plan for my life, but even today, whenever I speak in public, the butterflies are still there. The difference is that I've learned to feel the fear and move forward anyway. In the same way, your tenacity, when you are confronted with potentially disabling anxiety, will allow you to break through the barrier of fear. Maybe your fear is of public speaking; or you might have a fear of applying for a job in a new field, or talking to your son and daughter about sex. Your fear might be that of a single mom facing an unexpected pregnancy, or the challenge of raising a child with special needs. Whatever your situation, take the advice of my friend and remember that it's not about you. If you accept the fear, push through it, and reach for the next rung on the ladder, you'll be climbing upward. And you're sure to be helping others even as you move closer to your dreams.

Making You *a Priority*

A third common reason we moms fail to achieve our best is that we fall into the trap of giving until there's nothing left to give. We are nurturers at heart. We love our husbands and children fiercely, so when our families are in need—which can be any and every hour of the day—we do whatever it takes to support and care for them. Need a last-minute costume for the school play? Accidentally left your lunch at home? Suddenly sick and need someone to drop everything to watch over you? Mom will take care of it. Family means everything to us. We willingly give up our lives to serve our loved ones. Nothing is more rewarding to us. Even when we complain about it, we still do it.

This is a noble, loving attitude—to a point. The problem is that we moms frequently neglect our own needs, sometimes to an alarming degree. We ignore the signs telling us that we need to slow down, that we need to nurture our own souls. Most moms are sleep-deprived. We keep wishing we could plug ourselves into the wall like a refrigerator and renew our energy. Sadly, the plug isn't working, the current isn't flowing, and our systems are shutting down. How many of us, purely out of fatigue, lash out at family members? How often do we make choices we'll later regret because, at the moment, we're at our breaking point? How many of us are discouraged to the point of tears because we're too busy and too tired to be the moms we want to be every day?

This is a daily struggle for most of us. I don't always make taking care of myself a priority. What, after all, could be more important than caring for our children? What I've slowly come to realize is that I will only be the best I can be—including the best wife for my husband and mother for my children—if I take time for me. When I neglect my own need for rest, renewal, and growth, I'm neglecting my family, too. They deserve excellence from me, not half-frozen, leftover emotions.

Recently I was invited to speak during a televised international conference at the Crystal Cathedral in Garden Grove, California. The day of the scheduled visit came at an exceptionally stressful time for our family. Less than a month before, my husband's dad, Phil Olsen—a beloved husband, father, father-in-law, and grandpa—had passed away. A few days after that, Greg nearly died during a storm in the Channel Islands off the coast of California. I was dealing with challenges at the office and working to finish this book. It's always an honor to be invited by the Schuller family to the Crystal Cathedral. All of the Schullers are great people, and Dr. and Mrs. Schuller have become friends and mentors. They are living examples of the importance of honoring commitments. I wanted to speak at the conference and be at my best. I also needed to be available to my family at a time of crisis. I felt overwhelmed—I didn't know how I was going to make it.

The afternoon before the event, my mom walked into our kitchen. I was sitting at the table with my head in my hands. My wet cheeks and red nose weren't the result of a cold. "Kathy, what's the matter?" she asked. I didn't want to burden Mom. "Nothing," I said in a monotone voice. As I often do, I was trying to bury my feelings of sadness, pressure, and inadequacy. This time, though, my mom's question unleashed a voice of wisdom that broke through my mental fog. I saw in that instant that in my determination to give to everyone else, I was going to end up helping no one. I would be too stressed to support my family and wouldn't have time to properly prepare my speech. And so I did something that is very hard for me—I asked for help. I asked my mom if she would watch and spend time with our kids, and I arranged to spend the night at a relative's house so I could work on my speech. By not trying to do everything, an impossible situation suddenly became manageable. For me, it was the right solution.

I've come to realize that it's truly important to make "you" one of your priorities. If family really matters, remember that you're a member of your family. When you take care of yourself, your family will benefit more than you can imagine.

Real Solutions

PROBLEM: I do have a few dreams—one of them is to own my own business—but I'm so afraid of losing money, failing, and looking foolish that I don't want to try. Where do I find the courage to go for it?

SOLUTION: Allow yourself the freedom to fail.

Lucille Ball said, "Not everything that is faced can be changed, but nothing can be changed until it is faced." She also said, "It doesn't pay to get discouraged. Keeping busy and making optimism a way of life can restore your faith in yourself."[1] I believe she was on to something. If we allow our fear to overwhelm us to the point where we lose our optimism and willingness to try, we'll never stretch our abilities enough to develop new "muscles" that allow us to do more. Everyone loved Lucy. It's ironic to realize that the world's most famous funny lady never thought she was funny. Lucy always said she was brave.

I know of a man who encountered one setback after another. Over a period of twenty-seven years, he endured the death of his fiancée, two business failures, and a mental breakdown. During these years he also ran for public office but found disappointment there as well. He was rejected in his attempts to serve as state legislator, presidential elector, state land officer, congressional representative, U.S. senator (twice), and U.S. vice president.

The man's name was Abraham Lincoln. Following that string of failures, he was elected president of the United States. His determination held our nation together during one of the most turbulent times in its history. Today he is considered by many people to be our strongest and most admirable president. History books present Abraham Lincoln as a great leader but don't always mention the risks and rejections that led to his success.

The point is that it's okay to try and fall short. When you give yourself permission to fail, you can learn much. Successful people actually have more failures than anyone else because they're willing to make the attempt and gain from the experience. If you have a dream for your life, my advice is to go for it—and if it doesn't come together right away, ask yourself what you can change when you try again.

PROBLEM: I've always struggled to believe in myself. Even as a young girl, I felt that the other girls were smarter and prettier. I still feel that way. What can I do to stop feeling inadequate?

SOLUTION: Don't play the comparison game.

It's natural when we're young to look at our friends, people in the media, and classmates and decide where we rank in terms of popularity, value, beauty, and brains. As we grow, however, those comparisons can lead to trouble. Once you decide that everyone else is smarter, better, and more popular than you, that perception can become a self-fulfilling prophecy. And the longer you limit yourself with such negative thinking, the harder it will be to break the habit.

A woman named Isabel Wolseley once wrote about feeling that she didn't measure up during her senior year of high school. Her classmates had better clothes, more friends, better grades, and always seemed to know what they were doing. Isabel lived on a farm. Her family had less money than most of the families around her. She felt out of place.

Twenty years after graduating, Isabel overcame her feelings of inadequacy enough to attend a high school reunion. Once there, she was surprised to learn that many of her friends had felt just as inadequate as she did. As one put it, "You lived on a farm! You had a Shetland pony to ride. A haymow to play in. Now you're a writer and you travel all the time. I've always envied you!"[2]

I appreciate Isabel's story. When I was in junior high school, I didn't feel good about myself. I was an awkward girl with one thick eyebrow. If only I'd known about tweezers and conditioner for the helmet I called hair! I was lonely because I didn't have any friends. Classmates made fun of me all the time. Only when I realized and trusted that God loved me did I begin to see my true worth.

If you look hard enough, you'll always find someone else who is smarter, prettier, wittier, or wealthier. Instead of dwelling on the perceptions and circumstances of the people around you, why not thank God for the gifts and talents He's given you? Being negative about ourselves in relation to others can keep us in our uncomfortable comfort zone. Conversely, some of us belittle others with sarcasm in order to lift ourselves up at their expense. We say, "Well, I make mistakes, but I'm not as bad as . . ." Either choice will hinder you from fulfilling your own destiny. You are a unique individual designed by God. He sees you as one of His marvelous creations. That makes you worth celebrating!

PROBLEM: I'm not happy with my life right now, but I can't seem to find the motivation to do anything about it. How do I find hope?

SOLUTION: Find your hope in God.

It breaks my heart to see heaviness and hopelessness taking such a toll on moms. I know how the burdens of daily life can crush even the most optimistic spirit. Please remember that there's always hope! You may not be able to see the solutions to your life's problems right now, but they are out there. God has a plan for your life, and He will help you find the answers you need.

I love the Bible verse that reads, "We have this hope as an anchor for the soul, firm and secure" (Hebrews 6:19). That's the kind of anchor that won't hold us back but will give us wings to fly. Your soul and your future are secure with God. All of us can find great comfort and joy in those words. I don't mean to impose my faith on anyone. We all have free will, and you will make your own decisions about what you believe. I care about people and want them to be happy, to hope and dream and live life to the fullest. Give your burdens to God in prayer, and you'll be on your way.

Your Best You Solutions Checklist

- [ ] What were your dreams as a child?

- [ ] What are your dreams today?

- [ ] What steps are you taking to sweep away obstacles and pursue your dreams?

- [ ] Do you believe in yourself and your God-given value?

- [ ] Are you most often an "engine" or an "anchor"? Are you surrounding yourself with "engines"?

- [ ] Is fear disabling you, or are you pushing through the fear to achieve your goals and offer your best self to others?

- [ ] Are you taking care of yourself and your needs?

- [ ] Are you willing to fail and learn from your mistakes?

- [ ] Are you remembering to avoid comparisons with others?

- [ ] Do you draw hope not from current circumstances but from God's love and plans for your life?

chapter six

No *I* in *Mom*

So many diapers, so many dirty dishes,

so many demands. I had a life once.

Where did it go, and how do I get it back?

Mom, can you take me to soccer?" "Mom, what about my homework?" "Mom, can you be a Girl Scout leader this year?"

Mom. Such an interesting, powerful, beautiful word. It contains just three letters, yet it inspires countless images of love, devotion, sacrifice, and service. And if we examine the word closely, we see that among those three letters, *I* is nowhere to be found.

We moms seem to take that missing *I* to heart. Mothers across the country tell me that they are unconditionally committed to supporting and caring for their families but that they're collapsing under the strain. The higher they lift their loved ones, the further they drop into a sinkhole of despair. They have a deep desire to be amazing wives and moms but feel like failures because they don't have the strength to keep going. They're saying, "I need to be there for my family. They are the priority. I don't have time to take care of myself!"

I know this feeling well. As I shared earlier in this book, it took a pair of wakeup calls—the death by heart attack of a father I knew and the hard-to-hear but true words of a friend—to make me realize that I was neglecting my physical health and needed to make some changes. When it comes to choosing priorities, we moms tend to put our own needs at the bottom of the list. Sooner or later, that approach to life catches up with us.

Take the example of Kathy Peel, a respected author and family management expert. Years ago she was running hard, just like most moms I know. She had two active boys, ages nine and five, and was constantly shuttling them to practices, games, and other events. She almost always said yes to requests for help from family and friends. Her calendar was filled with one commitment after another. And she collapsed, exhausted, at the end of each day, realizing she hadn't enjoyed even five minutes of it.

One fateful day Kathy finally went too far. In addition to managing her own family, she attended two community service meetings, prepared and delivered dinner to a pair of new mothers, helped a friend highlight her hair, and assisted another friend with choosing and packing clothes for a trip.

The next day Kathy was in the hospital, "completely drained of energy and unable to think clearly or function without pain."[1] She was eventually diagnosed with chronic fatigue syndrome. In her efforts to serve everyone around her, Kathy had ignored her own needs and burned out. Suddenly she wasn't able to help anyone.

Too many moms are headed down this same road. They're so busy meeting the needs of others that their own fuel tanks are empty. These moms are ready to crash. Are you one of them? If ten minutes alone in the bathroom sounds to you like a dream vacation, the answer is yes.

Meet Your Needs

We moms fall into countless ways of neglecting our needs—seemingly small things that nonetheless eat into our schedule and take away time for ourselves. We may not even realize it's happening. Ask yourself if any of the following sound familiar:

- You agree without thinking to almost any request.

- You feel more like a maid than a mother to your children.

- You begin each day planning to exercise, to write that play, and to clean out the garage—but as soon as someone has a "crisis," you drop everything to rush to his or her aid.

- At the end of the day, you realize you never sat down.

- You're involved in volunteer or ministry projects that you have no interest in or enthusiasm for.

- You sometimes resent your family because they never notice how much you do for them or how they could help.

- Your career used to be rewarding, but now it just feels like another burden.

- Your strongest wish from the moment you get up in the morning is for the day to end so you can go to bed.

- You don't take time for God or for reflection on the deeper issues in life.

• You've set aside or forgotten about your goals and dreams.

Ouch. If you're anything like me, I'm guessing that a few of these are hitting the mark. Now, you may be ready to argue with me. You may feel that even though you're exhausted, you are needed, and this is what life as a mom is all about. These are sacrifices you're willing to make to serve your family and your business, church, or nonprofit organization. And yes, those are all worthy priorities. But you must be a priority too. If you push yourself nearly to the edge of your abilities, you'll be serving and performing at a level far below your best. And if you go beyond your limit, you'll soon shut down and won't be serving anyone. Think about this and you'll realize that taking care of yourself isn't a matter of being selfish. It's actually a precious gift to those you love.

It also may be true that you are unsatisfied with your life and don't want to feel drained every moment of the day, but you don't know what to do about it. You feel trapped by your circumstances. If you've been living this way for a while, it may be difficult to even imagine anything different. I assure you that you aren't trapped and that your life can change. It won't always be easy, and it won't happen overnight; but you have the power right now to choose a different path. Let's talk about a few practical steps that will get you started.

Recognize the Power of Words

The words we use can be a powerful influence on those around us. We've already discussed how our word choices may honor and build up our loved ones or tear them down. Simply the way you greet your husband and children can set the tone for the rest of their day. Your words will be equally significant in your new efforts to make yourself a priority.

One of the most powerful words in the English language consists of only two letters: *no.* We moms tend to shy away from using this word. It makes us feel self-centered, antisocial, and uncooperative. When the mother of our daughter's friend calls and asks if we can help with the elementary school Valentine's Day party next week, we think, *Next week? I've already committed to organizing the church rummage sale. How can I fit in a Valentine's Day party?* Yet for some reason, what comes out of our mouths is, "Sure, count me in."

Part of our reluctance to say no has to do with the way we're made. God created women to be nurturers and helpers, and it feels right to fulfill that role. Part of it is our innate desire to connect with others. We appreciate being valued enough to be invited and want to participate. Part of it is simply habit. When others ask, we don't hesitate. By the time our brains have engaged, the "yes" is already in the air.

God has also instructed us, however, to be wise: "Blessed is the man who finds wisdom. . . . She [wisdom] is more precious than rubies" (Proverbs 3:13, 15). Where's the wisdom in taking on more than we can handle? What does it say about our judgment and reliability if we agree to commitments we can't keep? Remember, any time that you add another activity to your schedule, you're taking away from something else. It's more than okay to say no if someone else's request doesn't line up with your priorities. In fact, it's essential if you want to live a life of excellence.

One of the toughest lessons I've had to learn as a mom is that "no" is a complete sentence. So often, when asked to do something, we moms follow "no" with what sounds like an apology: "No, I'd better not; my husband keeps complaining that I never spend time with him"; "No, I would, but my son is having trouble in one of his classes, and I should help him with his homework"; "No, I want to, but I haven't slept well all week, and I'm just really tired." You don't need to apologize, and you don't need an excuse. "No" is all that's necessary (though adding "thank you" never hurts).

Another way our words can help us change the way we take care of ourselves is what I call finding your voice. A movie critic once wrote that I had a voice that could kill small animals. I was hurt by this comment, but it did make me listen more closely to my speaking voice. It may be time for you to listen to your voice too—the one inside that is too often drowned out by others' priorities. What whispers from the deepest part of your soul have you ignored? What needs have you neglected? When we stuff down our feelings, they usually reappear in other, unhealthy forms such as anger, overeating, or depression. Find some quiet time and truly listen to what your mind and body are telling you. One thing I bet you'll hear is that you need to be a better friend to yourself.

Don't stop there, though. It's time to use that rediscovered voice. Schedule a time to talk with your husband and children. Tell them how you're feeling, and let them know what you need from them in order to change that. Don't complain; just communicate. If you've stored up a warehouse full of resentment, this may not be easy. Keep in mind that this is your family, and they really are on your side. They may not even be aware of how deeply their actions (or lack of actions) have affected you. Be persistent—one conversation probably won't be enough. Remember the power of words, and seize the opportunity to make them work for you.

Renew and Recharge

You already know that I love to walk, bicycle, swim, and surf. I'm aware that these activities are good for my body, but they are more to me than methods of fitness. Getting my body moving in the outdoors is just plain fun, especially when my family is involved. I've learned that this is one of the ways I recharge my batteries and counteract the stressful demands of life.

I recharge in lots of other ways too. Talking with family and friends, hanging out with Greg and our children, attending church, and going to women's retreats are all things that renew and invigorate me. Recently I've begun setting my alarm clock fifteen minutes to an hour earlier. I spend that extra morning time studying the Bible and talking with and listening to God. Starting each day by focusing on Him has made a huge difference in my life. When I don't make time for God, my priorities seem to get out of alignment, and I have more trouble coping. When I do set aside time, He gives me the strength and peace to find solutions for the challenges that continually arise. I've discovered that focusing on God is a way to care for myself.

These are the things that work for me, the activities that soothe and restore my soul. Though crises inevitably interrupt my plans on some days, I have dedicated myself to consistently including these rejuvenating activities in my daily life. I need them in order to be the person I want and am meant to be.

Have you taken the time to identify what refreshes and energizes you? Even if you're sure you already know, stop right now and list on paper or computer ten things that bring joy and renewed strength into your life. Go ahead—I'll wait.

All done? Let's look at your list. Some of your choices are probably easier to accomplish than others. Some may be more than your budget can accommodate at present. Some may take time you don't think you have. Here's the key question: when was the last time you engaged in each of these activities? If most of your answers fall into the categories of "last month," "last year," or "it's been so long I can't remember," you need to take action. You've heard of the iPod? What you need now is "iTime." Beside each item on your list, write out a brief plan that details how you can incorporate that wonderful energy-builder into your lifestyle. You enjoy exercise, music, quiet time, or a night at the movies? Maybe you know a friend who will trade off with you, watching each other's kids for an afternoon or evening. You'd love a weekend getaway with your hubby but can't afford it? Start saving for that goal today, and eventually it will become a reality.

I can't stress enough how important it is that you begin taking care of yourself *today*. You can start small: make it a priority to set aside at least fifteen minutes for yourself every morning and afternoon. Schedule it for a specific time so it doesn't get lost in the shuffle. If you have a full-time job outside the home, consider slotting your "iTime" in the morning and evening, or whenever makes the most sense for your schedule. The important thing is to commit to it. Once it's on your calendar, protect that time as you would a meeting with a long-lost friend—because you know what? You are meeting an old friend, one you probably haven't connected with for a long time. That friend is you.

Rediscover Your Dreams

We've all heard the term *stage mother.* I saw quite of a few of them during my career as a model—moms who attempted to live out their dreams through their children. It was never a healthy situation for either party. The child, often a daughter, was under tremendous pressure to succeed and do exactly what the mother wanted. The mom, guiding and pushing behind the scenes, had transferred her hopes for the future onto her unprepared offspring.

You probably aren't putting this level of pressure on your kids, yet it's more common than most people realize for moms to subconsciously give up their own dreams and live vicariously through their children. Of course we all have aspirations for our kids. We want them to find joy and success in life. But when a parent no longer makes plans for her own future and instead expects her child to provide the joy that's missing, she's made a recipe for trouble.

No matter how old we are or what circumstances we find ourselves in, we all need goals and dreams. God has created each of us with a passion to fulfill His purposes for our lives, yet we often dismiss those plans as too impractical or something that we'll take care of later. Some of us get so buried under our daily duties that we forget our passions and dreams altogether. If we neglect the very purposes for which we were created, we can't help feeling discouraged and feeling that something is missing. It's as if we have a hole in our hearts.

Remember the previous chapter, when you wrote down your dreams? Let's go back to that list. Are those still your desires for your future? Are there more goals you'd like to add? What needs to change in your life to turn these dreams into reality? You may want to pray about this before we go further.

Now take a few minutes and—just as you did for the "recharge list" above—write out a plan that will enable each of your dreams to come true. Set aside any doubts and excuses. Be willing to think big. Accept that most of your dreams will require sacrifice and an openness to change. Realize also, though, that once you set in motion the process of achieving your dreams and God's purposes for your life, you'll rediscover feelings you may not have experienced for a long time: joy and hope. Sometimes the journey to your dreams is just as rewarding as the dream itself.

Believe That You're Worth It

We've talked about several valuable steps that will help you take better care of yourself as a mother. They can make a huge difference in your life and enable you to move toward becoming the mom you were born to be. They're all based, however, on one essential ingredient that you cannot do without if you truly desire to make yourself a priority: you must believe you are worth it.

I know of a woman—I'll call her Julie to protect her privacy—who was unhappy with her life. Caring for three active boys left Julie exhausted and often near tears at the end of each day. Her husband was sympathetic when he was around, but he was so engrossed in his work that he didn't seem to notice Julie's deepening depression. Though she was miserable, Julie didn't feel she had the right to express her needs. When it came to her own feelings, she thought they didn't count. She figured that her role as a wife and mom was to take care of everyone else and "just live with it."

One day at the grocery store, a man Julie had met once or twice before struck up a conversation. She was flattered by his interest. They ran into each other a second time and talked longer. Julie never intended to have an affair, but her exhaustion and unhappiness left her in a vulnerable state of mind. She eventually divorced and remarried . . . and found herself more miserable than ever. She had traded one set of marriage problems for another, and now she deals with the added burden of guilt over the impact of her divorce on her children. No one can say for sure what would have happened had Julie spoken up to her family about her unhappiness. I do believe, though, that if she'd honored and respected herself enough to care for her own needs, she would have had a much better chance of establishing the kind of marriage and family she wanted.

We all have individual needs that must be respected. We all have a responsibility to care for ourselves. Even Jesus drew boundaries. Despite the great needs around Him, when crowds of people approached, seeking healing, He "often withdrew to lonely places and prayed" (Luke 5:16). If Jesus could postpone the needs of others in order to be alone, pray, and refresh, who are we to try to get along without doing the same?

Each of us is worthy of self-respect. Each of us counts. The Bible tells us that "we are God's workmanship, created in Christ Jesus to do good works, which God prepared in advance for us to do" (Ephesians 2:10). Does God do sloppy work? I don't think so. We also know that Jesus came to earth specifically to die for us (John 3:16). Would He have sacrificed Himself this way if He hadn't believed we were worth it? No again. The truth of the matter is that you are royalty. You may find it hard to think of yourself this way. But Jesus, the King of kings, has chosen you to be with Him for eternity. He has invited you to be part of His royal family (1 Peter 2:9).

Greg and I are inspired by our daughters. Our oldest daughter, Lily, went through a period of time when she especially enjoyed stories and movies about princesses. Our youngest, Chloe, is doing the same today. Chloe came to me one day and said, in a sad voice, "Mommy, I'll never be a real princess." She'd obviously thought hard about this. I took her onto my lap and spoke softly. "Oh, but you already are a princess, darling.

You are the ultimate princess because your Father in heaven is the King of kings."

I believe every mom is a princess. I don't mean that you need to play dress-up or wear a crown or step out of a golden carriage or find a glass slipper. I'm not saying that you need a prince to be a princess. Without any of that, you are royalty in God's eyes and should treat yourself with love and respect. There may not be an *I* in *mom*, but there certainly is in *princess*. Keep that in mind as you go through each day, and you may find that caring for yourself comes just a little bit easier.

Just for Dad

If you're a father reading this book, thank you for investing this time in your wife and family. This chapter is about helping the woman in your life take better care of herself so she can be all she was meant to be. Every person is responsible for taking care of his or her own needs, yet for many women, making their needs a priority is a challenge. Even though this is her responsibility, you, as her husband, most definitely can help.

No one knows your wife and what's going on in her life better than you do. You see her daily battles and what she's struggling with. You understand her strengths and weaknesses. If you're anything like most of the husbands I know, you love your wife dearly and would do anything for her. Yet you're grappling with challenges of your own, which often include career demands and fulfilling your role as Dad. You want to show your wife how much she means to you, but finding the time to do so seems to get tougher every year.

Believe me, as a business owner, I appreciate your dilemma. My encouragement to you is this: little gestures add up to a big, powerful love. You don't have to plan a dream vacation or buy her a diamond to communicate your feelings. It's the small things you do each day that will bring joy to her heart. Maybe it's offering to give her a foot massage before bedtime. Maybe it's grabbing the grocery list and doing the day's shopping. Perhaps it's taking the kids to the park for part of a Saturday afternoon so she can work out or simply have quiet time alone.

I'm reminded of the day I flew home from a business trip feeling awful. I was coughing and had a fever. It later turned out that I had pneumonia. The trip had not been successful in terms of my priorities. Besides my illness, there was another family illness and crisis going on. I'd planned to get a ride home from the airport with one of my partners, but when we landed there was Greg. He'd rearranged his busy schedule to meet me. I was so happy to see him, I burst into tears. A small thing, you say? Not to me. It was a loving act that touched my heart, and one I'll never forget.

You can care for your spouse in many ways. Work with her on disciplining the kids so that, as parents, you're consistent and united. Hold back the criticism if you don't like how she handled a situation in your absence. If you see her taking on more commitments than she can handle, lovingly ask if changes are needed and if you can help. Take five minutes each day to pray with her about whatever problems you each are facing.

The best advice of all on caring for your wife is found in Scripture: "Husbands, love your wives, just as Christ loved the church and gave himself up for her to make her holy" (Ephesians 5:25–26). The woman you married all those years ago still needs you to give yourself up for her. No matter how well we moms appear to be holding things together, there are times when we tremble inside. It's wonderful to know we can lean on the shoulder of the man we love.

Real Solutions

PROBLEM: I know I need to take better care of myself, and am trying to change, but it seems that little things keep stealing my time. How do I steal more of it back?

SOLUTION: Simplify.

It's common for people today to confuse complexity with success. When we're rushing from one appointment to another and filling our homes with possessions, we tend to feel more important. But what we don't realize is that often those appointments and items are robbing us of valuable time, energy, and money. Serving on the Little League board is a worthy cause, but are the evenings away from our families worth the price? The new widescreen TV or fancy stereo system is nice, but by the time we've redesigned the living room to accommodate the new equipment, taken the replaced items (which worked just fine) to the dump, read the operating manual, filled out the warranty registration, and visited the repair shop because a part broke in the first week, has it really been worth it?

Complexity is a destroyer. Simplicity is beautiful. If you apply that philosophy to your life, you may discover many ways to insert more time into your schedule. There's a hidden cost to every new activity and possession that you add to your life. Be willing to say no to a request for help or to a purchase you don't need.

You can take back time in other ways too. For instance, we've discussed how important it is to define your priorities and dreams. Figure out what you value, and put boundaries in place to protect you and your loved ones from time-eating, compromising, or dangerous situations. Boundaries needn't be complicated. As you know, I value our family time. When I'm at home, I screen my calls. Even people I love have to go to voice mail. I get back to them, I'm just not necessarily available on their timetable. That's a boundary that works for me.

Another simple solution for many families is to turn off the TV. I know how tempting it is after a long day to want to relax for a few minutes and be entertained. But those few minutes can easily turn into two hours, and suddenly your evening is lost. A short walk may be just as relaxing, includes the added benefit of exercise, and leaves the rest of the evening for you to address whatever needs to be done.

PROBLEM: I'm a mother with two teenage children. I realize that for years I haven't taken care of my own needs and that I've been angry at my family and said things I regret because of it. I want to change. How can I get those mistakes out of my head?

SOLUTION: Learn and let go.

We all have an inner critic, that negative voice that constantly reminds us of past mistakes and points out new ones. However, a mistake stays a mistake only if we don't learn from it. Successful people may stumble more than anyone else precisely because they are willing to try, fail, and grow as a result. We can't ignore the past, but when we listen to our inner critic, we allow old mistakes to hold us back. Think about the way your car is designed. You have a huge windshield that enables you to see everything in front of you. You also have a small rearview mirror that allows you to check on what's behind you. Obviously, you're going to be a more successful driver if you focus primarily on what's ahead. Yes, you need to glance back once in a while. There's valuable information there. But your windshield is many times larger than the rearview mirror for a reason.

Similarly, we all have past hurts and situations where others have let us down. We need to deal with those issues but not dwell on them. I don't mean that they should be swept under the carpet. Working through painful experiences will take time and effort. Yet if we honestly confront any wrongs we've suffered and can forgive—not condone but forgive—the people responsible, we'll be free from bitterness and able to look ahead to a brighter future.

God has something to say about this too. If you're drowning in guilt, He wants you to come to Him and ask for forgiveness: "If we confess our sins, he is faithful and just and will forgive us our sins" (1 John 1:9). And if you're holding on to any pain you've suffered in the past, it's time for you to do the forgiving: "If you hold anything against anyone, forgive him, so that your Father in heaven may forgive you your sins" (Mark 11:25). It's certainly not easy; but if God can forgive and forget, you can do the same.

PROBLEM: My husband and I just divorced. I'm suddenly responsible for three children, and I feel completely overwhelmed. I don't think I can do this on my own!

SOLUTION: Don't travel this road alone—seek help.

Motherhood is an incredible challenge for any woman, but doubly so for the single mom. It takes great skill and courage to raise a family when all the responsibilities that go with parenting and putting food on the table, as well as every other large and small decision, rest on your shoulders. For twenty years I've participated in a program through Athletes and Entertainers for Kids that offers scholarships and encourages young, single moms to build better lives. I have seen what these young women are up against, and I have incredible respect and admiration for them. Despite difficult circumstances, they are choosing to become responsible parents and adults.

If you are a single mom, I appreciate how frightening and overwhelming that can be. Please don't expect to do it all yourself! Everyone needs a support system, but it's especially critical for the single parent. You must be willing to reach out and seek help. Family and friends are obvious potential resources. So are wonderful programs such as the Boys & Girls Clubs of America, an organization our company has worked with and supported for many years. Your church may also be an excellent place to find help and support for you and your children. A women's Bible study group can be a great place to meet new friends who will listen to your concerns and share in your burdens. Likewise, many churches offer youth programs that are healthy places for your kids to make friends and grow their faith.

Financial issues tend to be another huge challenge for single moms. You may not be used to handling the family finances. You may not have the job or training to earn the dollars you need to support your family. You may not have a job at all. Find out about budgeting classes and job opportunities through the Internet and through people you know. If you need further education, ask if the colleges in your area offer scholarships for single moms—many do. Check out the national grant programs that are available for single parents. The process may seem daunting, but if you're persistent, you will find the help you need.

The issue that may concern you the most as a single mom is simply your ability to be an effective parent for your kids. Again, I encourage you to seek help as you raise your children. Look for positive role models who can interact with them and share some of the load, and don't exclude men from your search. Screen everyone carefully, of course, before you trust them with your precious young ones. Realize also that mentors can be a wonderful blessing for your family.

Finally, I urge you to look for ways to take care of yourself as you meet all of these challenges. I know it is terribly hard. If you are a person of faith, remember to draw on the Lord when circumstances seem bleak. Consider these words from Scripture: "You hear, O LORD, the desire of the afflicted; you encourage them, and you listen to their cry" (Psalm 10:17). You are not alone.

Taking Care of Mom
Solutions Checklist

☐ Review the checklist at the beginning of the chapter. Are you taking care of your needs, or are you running on empty?

☐ Are you saying no when you need to?

☐ What is your inner voice telling you about your life and schedule?

☐ Are you voicing your needs to your family?

☐ What have you done in the last week to recharge your batteries?

☐ How are you planning to recharge in the week ahead?

☐ What steps are you taking to move closer to realizing your goals and dreams?

☐ In what ways could you simplify your life?

☐ Are you looking through your windshield at the opportunities in front of you, or are you more focused on the mistakes in your rearview mirror?

☐ Do you view yourself with self-respect, as royalty? Remember, you are a daughter of the King!

chapter seven

Faith and Your Family

I believe in God. I just don't seem to have

time for church and the Bible and all that.

Does an active faith really make such

a difference?

*O*ne of the greatest compliments I receive is when people ask how I cope with all the stresses and demands in my life and still have everything together. It's a compliment, but the perception isn't true. No matter what the appearance, only God controls the present and the future. I don't know what tomorrow holds. I do know, however, who holds tomorrow. From the time I was eighteen, I've leaned on a loving best friend to be there for me, listen to me, love me, and protect me. I'm ashamed to admit that I haven't always been there for Him. He's always there for me. That friend is Jesus Christ.

Shortly after graduating from high school, during the early days of my modeling career, I traveled to Paris. I stayed in the apartment of someone I worked with, in a room at the end of a long hallway, which I later learned was known as "the dungeon." In the middle of one of those first nights in the dungeon, I woke up and couldn't get back to sleep. This was before the days of cell phones, iPods, and laptop computers. There was little to do.

My mom, who'd become a Christian just the year before, had packed a Bible in my bag. Out of boredom, jet leg, and loneliness, I picked it up, not knowing the Old Testament from the New Testament. Our family rarely attended church and had never owned a Bible. Though I believed in God, I had many more questions about Him than answers. I opened the Bible from Mom to the gospel of Matthew. The Word and the truth touched my heart, and my life was forever changed.

As a lonely young woman far from home, beginning a career too often dominated by men of questionable character, I was especially encouraged to see how Jesus honors women. He spoke with a Samaritan woman at a well even though Jews (Jesus was from a Jewish family) did not associate with Samaritans. When a crowd wanted to stone a woman caught in the act of adultery, Jesus did not condemn her. Instead, He released her and told her to leave her sins behind. After His death on the cross, He revealed Himself first to a woman. Jesus was a brave rebel: even though women did not have equal standing with men at that time, He treated women with great kindness and respect.

That night in the dungeon was the beginning of my unconditional and complete love for, belief in, and path toward obedience to Jesus. Now, I placed needless obstacles in that path, because I'm a pretty stubborn person. Even though I'd made a new best friend who would love and guide the rest of my life, I remained a "baby Christian" for too long. Reading through the Bible, I would pick and choose what to apply to my life. Some passages were great. Others I thought either didn't pertain to me or must have contained typos. I was guilty of trying to mold God into what I wanted Him to be rather than allowing Him to mold me into the person I was born to be.

Since that night in the dungeon, I've come a long way on

my spiritual journey—and I still have a great distance to travel. I pray that God will bless me with fruitful years so that I might serve Him. My heart is full, and I enjoy this personal relationship with my Lord and Savior. He is the focus and first love of my life. He brings comfort, peace, purpose, and joy to me and to my loved ones. We would be lost without Him.

If you haven't already, please accept God's invitation to discover His incredible blessings. Don't lose out by closing your ears or hardening your heart to the truth. Just as I was for so many years, you may be a Christian who finds ways to be less than fully committed to the Lord. You may not believe in God at all. I won't tell you what to believe, and I certainly don't expect you to alter your faith because of mine. Yet I do hope that you will take a clear and honest look at the love, truth, and life-changing power God offers. From my perspective, nothing is more important for you and your family than developing a powerful and personal relationship with the Lord.

Imagine Jesus seeing a movie of our life. Not just all the wonderful things we've done. Not just the mediocre stuff. Imagine Him watching a movie that shows everything, including our worst moments and thoughts. Kind of uncomfortable, right? Now consider this: Jesus lived the events of that movie with us. He knows every scene and every line by heart—and He loves us anyway, completely and unconditionally. How amazing, wonderful, and forgiving is that? He knows everything about us and everything that's in our hearts and minds—including the bad stuff—and He still surrounds and protects us with His love.

The more time I spend with the Lord, the more I realize how much I need Him. Some people see that as weakness.

They call it using a crutch. I admit it—I want and desperately need God's love as my support as I walk through life. When I try to handle things on my own, I mess up. Often I don't like what I do or what comes out of my mouth. When I ask Him to guide me and to help me speak His words, however, a potentially horrible dilemma can just melt away. Many times what I need to do is just shut up and pray. Sometimes I think I must have bite marks on my tongue because there's so much I want to say but don't. When I pray and listen for God's answer, He gives me the discernment to know what words to use and when to be quiet. With His way, the outcome is always different and always for the best.

Passing On the Faith

For my husband and me, and for millions of families, introducing our children to the Lord and allowing them the opportunity to develop a personal relationship with Jesus is a high priority. It may be a priority for your family too. So how do we pass on our faith to our children? How do we communicate this gift of faith that will change their lives both today and for eternity?

We can start with commitment and consistency. Moses said, "Impress them [God's commandments] on your children. Talk about them when you sit at home and when you walk along the road, when you lie down and when you get up. Tie them as symbols on your hands and bind them on your foreheads. Write them on the doorframes of your houses and on your gates" (Deuteronomy 6:7–9). It's more than taking our kids to church or saying a prayer at the end of the day. We must continually seek opportunities to teach our kids about God.

We also need to understand that it's never too soon to begin this instruction. When our kids learn early on that Jesus is their most amazing, most powerful, and most loving Savior, they'll be better equipped to deal with the fears, anxieties, and challenges that will come their way. And it's a lesson that's likely to stay with them for the rest of their lives. Scripture promises us, "Train a child in the way he should go, and when he is old he will not turn from it" (Proverbs 22:6).

Choosing a Church

Early in my faith life, stubbornness and disobedience limited my spiritual growth. During those years I didn't believe it was necessary to belong to a church. I read the Bible, I believed in God, I had a relationship with the Lord. Why commit time I didn't really have to hang out with people I didn't know?

I realize now how important finding a "home" church truly is for strength and growth. The Bible says, "You are the body of Christ, and each one of you is a part of it" (1 Corinthians 12:27). When we worship and spend time with people who are on the same spiritual journey, we discover new resources for support, understanding, and accountability. We come together and lean on one another. We ask and find answers to the problems that can't be resolved on our own. Each of us has something to give to the body of Christ. And we can receive even more.

How do you choose a church that will meet the spiritual

needs of you and your family? For our family, the first step is asking if the Bible is viewed as the Word of God and if the focus is on reading the Bible. You'll want more than stories and entertainment. Check out the youth programs that will minister to your kids. Will this be a place that your children can get excited about? Does it have leaders and mentors who will play a positive role in your children's lives? Are there programs and opportunities for kids to get together at times other than Sunday mornings? It's also wise to ask if your prospective church has an open-book policy on its budget. Good stewardship is one sign of a church that's on the right path.

Most of all, trust your intuition. When you walk in the doors, do you feel the presence of the Holy Spirit? Do you feel called upon to make a difference here? If you don't have a sense of peace about your experience, pray about it and discuss it with your family, and if you can't find answers that bring you peace, it's time to consider another church.

The Power of Prayer

A living faith in God is about more than believing in Him and going to church. It's an ongoing relationship, and that takes time. It's important to schedule times to pray, to study God's Word, and to listen to His voice. That's what a relationship is—talking and listening. As I mentioned, recently I've been setting my alarm clock to sound earlier so I can start my day by spending time with the Lord. That makes such a difference. You may find other times that work better for you—maybe during a break time at home or the office or just before going to bed.

The main thing is to keep the lines of communication open. As with any relationship, it only works if you make it a priority and put in the effort.

I've found that my communication with God doesn't happen only when it's convenient or on my schedule. I may be drifting off to sleep or wake up in the middle of the night and sense God nudging me to pray. Even if I'm tired, I try to be obedient to those nudges. Those are times to get out of bed and onto my knees. It's amazing that God values us so much that He wants us to play a role in His purposes through our prayers. He doesn't *need* our help. He *invites* us to join Him.

Sometimes God nudges us to pray for a person who is giving us grief. It may be a coworker, a family member, or a neighbor. That's not always easy, but believe that God knows what He's doing. Your prayers may be desperately needed: you may be the only one praying for that person. And you'll find yourself blessed too. Every time you feel a flash of anger toward that person, you can turn it into a prayer and ask God to bless him or her. It's a great way to dissolve the bitterness that can take root in your heart.

Prayer is incredible. It's a link to the power of our Father in heaven, and it's always available to us. A woman at our church was telling me, with tears in her eyes, about her adult son who was struggling with a chemical dependency. She said it was breaking her heart, that she'd tried everything, and there was nothing more she could do. I said, "Please don't underestimate the power of a praying mom. It's something strong you can always do and that will make a difference."

Through prayer, I am constantly reminded that no problem is too big for God to handle or too small for Him to be concerned about. Recently our family was on its way home from a trip and was trying to catch a connecting flight. The airline had lost our luggage. Greg went searching in one direction while one of our children and I headed off in another. Suddenly I stopped and thought, *Wait a minute. We haven't prayed about this.* God is limitless. He cannot be distracted. No prayer goes unanswered, even if we don't receive the answer we want. To some people, praying for help in this situation might seem silly or burdensome. I respectfully disagree. I encourage you to take action and pray over all things, big and small. We offered a prayer for God's help right there in the airport. As soon as we finished, we looked up, and there was Greg, coming our way and carrying my big red suitcase.

Ten minutes later we reached the gate for our connecting flight and found out we were too late to board. The woman behind the counter said she'd get us on the next flight. This time we remembered to pray right away. As we said "Amen," the airline official approached and said she could get us on the flight after all.

I was thankful and encouraged. I was also pleased to see our children's faith grow as they experienced God's answers to our prayers. Later I saw more evidence of our kids' developing faith when they offered a beautiful prayer for their beloved Grampa, who was ill and in the hospital. There's nothing quite like the joy of watching your son or daughter make a connection with the Lord. It's pure and uncomplicated. Children have a wonderful ability to relate to God and His Word. Let me encourage you to use the power of prayer to help your children grow closer to Him.

The Eye of the Storm

As I've said, my husband is an emergency room physician and commercial fisherman. We joke that when he's not saving lives, he's killing lobsters. (Greg says that's not true. He says he provides lobsters with luxurious accommodations and sends them on trips around the world; what happens to them after that is up to their future hosts.) On an evening before Christmas in 2007, Greg was fishing in the Channel Islands off the coast of California while I drove one of our children to join friends at a movie. I was feeling a little anxious. I made a few business and personal calls but still couldn't shake the feeling of discomfort.

I was in my car when the phone rang. It was the Coast Guard. They had received a distress signal from my husband's boat. I knew Greg was fishing alone that night. The Coast Guard official said it was probably a false alarm. I wanted to be reassured by that, but I wasn't. My anxiety grew as I remembered Greg saying I should take it seriously if the alarm ever went off, because he would never let it happen accidentally. Only two days before, we had buried Greg's beloved father, the best father-in-law I could ask for. My brain couldn't process this new escalating fear. I knew we needed God more than ever.

As I talked with the Coast Guard, a radio call came through in the background. Over the phone connection, I could hear Greg's voice, reassuring, strong, and clear. "I'm cold," he said. "Would someone please come and get me?" I was relieved by his calm tone. He explained that he was stranded on Santa Rosa Island. I thanked God for Greg's safety and was eager to have my husband home. It was a frightening moment, but it seemed that everything was under control.

Prayer can happen at any and every moment. I began praying the instant I learned about the crisis. Hearing Greg's voice was an answer to one of my ongoing prayers. During all the conversations to come with the Coast Guard and with family and friends, my most important dialogue was with God.

After we heard from Greg, the Coast Guard official said that a helicopter was on its way. He also explained how the weather conditions in the Channel Islands had suddenly turned rough that night. Even with the belief that Greg was safe and on his way home, I knew our family needed to lean on God and loved ones. As a form of coping and perhaps a need to be proactive, I began reaching out for help that thankfully was available. My mom stepped in to look after our children. Our close friends Dale and Julia were angels. Dale drove to the airport to meet me, and Julia stayed on the phone with me, guiding me to a part of the airport I'd never seen.

In the crisis that night, despite my strong faith, I still felt a certain amount of fear. I was having a hard time finding where Greg would land. Yet God sent angels to lead us and protect us. Dale, who owns a local restaurant, lovingly and thoughtfully brought food and fellowship. I called loved ones and asked them to pray for Greg's health and safe return. Those loved ones called other people of many faiths. Within minutes, more people than we could count were praying for my husband's life and for our family. As my mom, Dale, and Julia showed, prayer can be accompanied by action. Each person knows what he or she did that night. My family's gratitude for each prayer and each action is forever. We thank you all.

The weather where Greg was fishing was worse than anyone imagined, and it kept changing. The rising tide had swept Greg's boat, which had been beached, back out to sea. When the Coast Guard helicopter approached, the boat was pitching violently in the high surf. There was no sign of Greg and no response to radio calls. When no evidence of life is visible and boarding a vessel poses a risk to Coast Guard rescuers, they are expected to stay clear.

From the helicopter the Coast Guard spotted Greg's survival bag on the beach, but no Greg. A rescuer was lowered by basket to the beach, and for an hour the search for Greg continued. The rescuer combed the island. For the last fifteen minutes, he stared from the beach through night-vision goggles at the pitching boat and wondered if Greg could be on board. Coast Guard rescues can be attempted for only so long. The rescuers were running out of fuel. Greg was running out of time. For those fifteen final minutes, the rescuer strategically evaluated the situation. The decision had to be made—how and if he should board the boat.

Finally, with the helicopter nearly out of fuel, this brave rescuer plunged into the icy cold ocean, fought the waves and the rocking boat, and courageously climbed aboard. At first he thought the boat was empty. Something we believe to be God's will caused this courageous man to continue searching. At the bottom of the boat, which had taken on water, he found Greg curled in a fetal position. His eyes were wide open, but there was no movement. Greg appeared to be dead. When the rescuer found a slight pulse, he realized that Greg was in a coma. Doctors later theorized that my husband had slipped and cracked his head against the boat and that carbon monoxide poisoning may have played a role in the crisis. Working against time and Greg's steadily dropping pulse, the rescuer maneuvered him into a hanging basket. More rescuers hauled Greg into the helicopter, and they flew off to the airport.

Unaware of the life-threatening status of the emergency, Dale and I arrived at the airport and noticed an ambulance. A kindly airport employee acknowledged the presence of the ambulance calmly. "Just routine," she assured us. We ran out with joy to the tarmac, expecting a happy reunion and a very different scene from the one we found. Greg's situation was urgent and critical. Paramedics and rescuers exchanged vital information amid the chaos. I clearly remember a wonderful man called Noodles urgently communicating with the paramedics: "Male, unknown identity, unconscious. There is a heartbeat. I don't know if he broke his neck. I couldn't keep him still." While these professionals fought to save Greg's life, Dale and I continued our prayers and sped behind the ambulance to join him in the hospital. I called family and friends to give updates and beg for prayer. Eventually, as the battery died on my cell phone, it allowed me to be at one with and to lean on the Lord.

I played in my mind the movie of Greg's and my life together. I remembered the silly squabbles every married couple has. In my mind's eye I saw Greg and I criticizing each other with our children in our midst . . . his business struggles . . . my business struggles. Differences that make no difference. I thought, *Wait a minute. None of this is important. I just want us to live in the Lord, raise our children, and be together. With those things in place, everything else better just fall in line.* It brought me back to the reality of what I cherish about the man I married and chose to be father of our children and spend eternity with. I just wanted my husband back.

Some of our loved ones were at the hospital, and some were on the phone, waiting, waiting, waiting. As our countless prayers continued, we watched the life return to Greg's body. It was a miracle. Doctors later told us that if he'd remained on the boat another twenty minutes, he wouldn't have survived the hypothermia. When Greg was able to speak, I asked, "Darling, what happened?" He quipped, "Honey, I got beat up." Only when I saw that Greg still had his sense of humor did I feel relieved and realize that he was going to be okay.

We believe that the prayers of many people around the world—family, friends, members of the fishing community, people at schools, churches, and hospitals—made the difference in Greg's rescue and recovery. When we called on God, He was there to guide and protect our family.

We'll never know what would have happened that night if so many people hadn't prayed. We do know we were on a collision course with tragedy, and Jesus intervened. I don't understand why our all-powerful Lord intervenes in some situations and not in others. I only know that we must find grace and gratitude in His decisions, whatever they are. I understand that some people, because they perceive my family member's lives to be more comfortable than theirs, may feel that it's easy for us to view God this way. My answer to that is that God's Word tells us to find joy even in our trials. The crisis I've just relayed is a beautiful illustration of a trial that ended in joy. Many other crises in our lives have not had joyous outcomes. Yet God remains our Rock, no matter what.

Greg is active in our community and shares his faith openly.

Recently, when speaking at a local church, Greg said, "I don't know why I was saved. I know there's a reason. If God allows me, through this situation, to help even one person, I am grateful. I want to make a difference. I wouldn't trade that accident for anything." Afterward, a woman came up to him, sobbing. She was hurting. She said his message had helped her and that she was that "one person." In truth, my husband—my hero—helps many people every day. And that's just one reason He is the love of my life.

If you believe in the Lord and cultivate a relationship with Him, He will be there for you and your family—during the good times and during the crises that inevitably will come your way. The Bible says that "the gift of God is eternal life in Christ Jesus our Lord" (Romans 6:23). He offers that wonderful gift to you and your loved ones every moment of every day, no matter what. My prayer is that you will receive it with joy.

Real Solutions

PROBLEM: I pray often for my family and others I know. Sometimes I feel that it isn't enough—that I should be doing more.

SOLUTION: Combine prayer with action.

Prayer is always a great first response to any problem or situation. It's our opportunity to communicate with our heavenly Father and call on His power and wisdom. It's vital, though, that we not allow prayer also to be our last response. Sometimes God will intervene and remove the problem we face. It's equally possible that, if we're listening for the answer to our prayers, we'll sense a directive to take action. Then it's up to us to move forward in obedience.

As always, Jesus is our perfect example. During His days on earth, He prayed often for His disciples and for the lost people He encountered. He didn't simply pray and wait for God to act, though. Jesus was and is involved in an active ministry filled with works, service, and compassion. We sometimes focus only on His acts of healing and divine miracles; but it's helpful for us to also notice—and follow—His examples of kindness, compassion, respect, feeding the hungry, protecting children, battling hypocrisy. Jesus's willingness to sacrifice His young life for all of us is an amazing inspiration.

Sometimes it's easy to focus on what we cannot do rather than step out and do what we must. When it was time to move ahead, Jesus did not hesitate to obey His Father. Neither should we.

PROBLEM: I've always believed that our church pastor is wonderful. Lately I've heard some rumors about him. I feel betrayed. It's even made me reconsider my faith. Is that wrong?

SOLUTION: Set your sights on Jesus.

People with honest hearts will sometimes fall victim to dishonest gossip. If you have questions about your pastor or anyone else, gently, lovingly, and respectfully confront that person. All that is necessary for ugliness to propagate is for it to go unanswered. We must not let people assassinate the character of others without those people being given an opportunity to defend themselves. It's also important that mortal deeds not disrupt our relationship with the Lord. One certainty in addition to God's love is human failure. People we love and who love us are going to disappoint us. Sometimes we will disappoint others. We can't help it. We need God. Though we all are made in His image, none of us is perfect. That includes leaders of every shape, size, color, belief, and gender. We can be role models when our behavior is at one with our beliefs. We still will fail.

Even our most-respected religious leaders are human. All you have to do is look at some of the larger-than-life figures in the Bible—Moses, Abraham, Noah, David, Peter—and you'll see that they each made mistakes. It's fine to admire, respect, and be inspired by people. It's also so important to be discerning. You may agree with them on one point; that doesn't mean you should agree with them on everything. It's always dangerous to put someone on a pedestal. Pastors are fallible. Like all of us, they fall short of the standard set by Jesus.

Please don't confuse human imperfection with the unshakable truth, wisdom, and love of our Lord. You can always count on Him. Even when I learn disturbing things about people I love, I choose to pray for them.

Never accept abuse, but be careful not to allow human frailties to destroy your relationships with loved ones. I love something that Jaclyn Smith's mother, Margaret Smith, once said: "If you look for a perfect friend, you'll never find even one." With the exception of Jesus, I believe that with all my heart. Gossip is a destroyer. Confront the victim of it as well as the person who is speaking it.

One great solution: stop the gossiper midstory and say, "Let me go and get the person you're talking about so we can have a constructive conversation." If that happens, you've made a positive change for good, whatever the response.

PROBLEM: My husband and I are believers, and so are our parents. I wonder, though, if our faith is taking root in our kids. How do we know if we're doing this right?

SOLUTION: Form an intelligent faith.

Here's something to think about. I recently attended a conference that featured Christian author and speaker Josh McDowell. He challenged parents in the audience with this statement: "You turned out okay. But if you raise your kids the same way your parents raised you, your kids aren't going to make it. It's a very different world."

Kids today are exposed to many different belief systems.

We can't expect our children to embrace our faith and values simply because we believe in them. Our kids are smart. We need to have an intelligent faith and be able to defend our beliefs. You are a role model to your children, and you must set a consistent and Christian example. It's also important to understand what and why you believe—and to share that in a meaningful way with your kids.

Faith and Family
Solutions Checklist

☐ Where are you in your faith journey? Where would you like to be?

☐ What steps are you taking to strengthen your faith?

☐ What obstacles are blocking you from the relationship you'd like to have with Jesus?

☐ What are you doing to introduce your children to Jesus?

☐ Do you attend church regularly? If not, why not? When will you start?

☐ Do you consistently spend time with the Lord? If not, what needs to change in your life to make this possible?

☐ Do you take your problems to God in prayer?

☐ Are you encouraging your children to do the same?

☐ Are you combining prayer with action?

afterword

Mom to Mom

*I*n this book we've identified solutions and resources to help us moms and our families live the lives of our dreams. We've talked about finances, building a happy home, health, safety, becoming our best, how to balance caring for others with caring for ourselves, and faith. Please use the checklists at the end of each chapter to help you stay on course. I'll be doing that too, and I'd love to learn which ones are most helpful to you.

This material is the foundation for a new beginning. It has progressed from my thoughts, research, and actions to a much more powerful place—your hands and your life!

Motherhood is such a responsibility and challenge, and such a privilege. Remember to celebrate the wonderful moments along the journey. Believe, as you move forward, that you are the best person for the job. God created you specifically for the role of mom in your family. There is only one you. You possess a unique combination of gifts and talents, and you are amazing! You cannot be replaced.

When your journey begins to feel overwhelming, I hope you'll turn to this guide for help. If you are blessed to know the

Lord, I hope you'll lean on Him. When you ask Him to, He will guide, protect, and help you. Many of the loved ones in your life also want to help you. Please don't pretend that you don't need help at times. We all do. I want to help you, too. Please contact me at www.kathyireland.com if you have a question, concern, or want to give me much-needed advice. We are not alone. We belong to a powerful group. We are moms.

Thank you for the honor of allowing me to share with you through this book. May God shower you and your family with His peace, joy, and blessings.

Love,
kathy

Closing Thoughts

As we finish this book, our country and our world face a devastating financial crisis. In the past, crises such as the Great Depression inspired us to establish a number of social programs. Today, however, many people are falling through those safety nets and are still struggling to meet the needs of their families. Before, millions experienced tremendous hunger, material loss, and financial suffering. Today, in addition to confronting some of these same issues, we must also deal with a heightened awareness of problems due to 24/7 news cycles, higher expectations, the "possession obsession" that we discussed earlier in this book, and a sense of entitlement. Our psyches are not as prepared to deal with economic challenges as our grandparents' were. Sadly, it is harder for us to give up what we have, whether it's the cell phone, the iPod, or the concept of living beyond our means.

If we do live beyond our means, we may be forced into desperate situations. There are many ways to become bankrupt, not only financially, but also emotionally and spiritually. What is the best way to deal with this frightening new reality? It may be no coincidence, and in many ways a blessing, that many of the solutions in this book were written to prepare us for this kind of situation. The current crisis reaffirms the fact that the only real security in life comes from our faith. The faith given to us by our Lord and Savior Jesus Christ is the one thing that can never be taken away. Our material possessions, our appearance, even the relationships we cherish are temporary. It is so important to appreciate the perspective that while we should do everything we can to recover our financial footing, we must put our hope for security and stability in the only absolute certainty in life, which is God's love. If ever there was a time to reorder our priorities and put God first, it is now.

The federal government is more deeply involved in our financial affairs and institutions than ever before. We've seen companies that people believed to be invulnerable giants crumble into dust. Our own company has dealt with corporations that sadly have experienced bankruptcy. But we can rebuild by keeping our spirits strong. Your circumstances, as bleak as they may seem today, are not permanent. This crisis may be your call to action, an opportunity to utilize some of the suggestions in the first chapter of this book. Things that may once have seemed unnecessary—a downsizing, a relocation, a more aggressive savings program, negotiating with your lenders—may now be precisely the steps required to turn your situation around.

No matter what economic stratum you live in, this is a time for belt-tightening. For such a long time, our country has been credit driven. Now credit is much, much tighter. As we said earlier in the book, it's like trick-or-treating. We thought we'd get a lot of goodies for free, but instead the trick is on us. For too long, we've believed that we could have things we really couldn't afford. We also said earlier in this book that people who acquire wealth do so by living far beneath their means. If you want to explore this idea further, I recommend the book *The Millionaire Next Door* (you can check it out of your library or order an inexpensive copy online). If you are continuing to display your wealth in order to impress others, you're probably not accumulating anything.

In light of the uncertainty about our finances, I encourage you to go back to the opening "Money Matters" chapter of this book and review it often. Keep in mind the key points, including:

- Negotiate, negotiate, negotiate.

- Check on the valuation of all your assets.

- Remember that maintaining a home is expensive, perhaps costing you 30 percent of its total value annually. You may want to consider moving to a less expensive location and turning your current home into a rental property.

Though this is a difficult time, there is also a beauty in it. I am reminded of this Scripture: "Consider it pure joy, my brothers, whenever you face trials of many kinds, because you know that the testing of your faith develops perseverance" (James 1:2–3). With the difficulty you are facing now, there can be no embarrassment, no shame, in changing your lifestyle to make it work for you and your family. In fact, just the opposite! You will find it a joy to break free of the chains that have kept you in a prison of debt and anxiety over finances.

I was so humbled to learn recently about a special mom. This woman does not consider herself or her family poor, but she allocates every penny. She literally lines up what her family's food program is going to be on a weekly basis. She has taken difficult circumstances and turned them into opportunities. In addition to having her children participate in planning the family food budget, she is also helping them cut back on unwanted and unhealthy calories. This mom is replacing the time she used to spend driving her kids somewhere to buy fast food snacks with physical, fun activities for her family. She and her children are spending less money and discovering more joy.

Though I don't presume to speak for God or to know all of God's plans, this terrible credit crunch and awful pain we're going through could very well be a wonderful blessing that gets us back on target to becoming a nation of favor and a nation of planners. As a nation, we've forgotten how to save and how to sacrifice. We have forgotten how to step back and ruthlessly evaluate every priority. We need to start asking ourselves a few important questions: Where do we want to live? How do we want to live? What do my family and I really need? How can we be successful?

The key at this moment in history may be to restore our hearts and spirits to a simpler lifestyle and simpler values. With the information overload and complexity we all experience today, we need to look for new ways to protect ourselves and our families. Maybe you've lost a significant portion of your retirement funds and college education savings for your kids. Okay. Dry your tears. Take a deep breath. Look in the mirror and say, "How are we going to live today so we can have a better life tomorrow?" Before you make a new purchase, ask yourself, "Why do I want this? How important is this? Do I really need this? Do I really care about it?" Each new possession brings with it an obligation and responsibility to care for it, even if it's just dusting it. How can you remove the clutter of things you really don't care about or need so you can live your joy and your passion?

When I have the joy of working with acclaimed landscape designer Nicholas Walker of J du J and he gets ready to design a beautiful garden, he talks about clearing the canvas. Today's financial crisis is a great opportunity for American moms to clear the canvas and plant seeds of love for our children.

You don't have to share my Christian faith to understand that anything that is material can disappear tomorrow. An economic collapse, a flood, an earthquake, a fire—so much can happen to put your financial holdings and possessions at risk. Those things will never give you a true sense of security. If you feel good about yourself, your family, your children, and your faith, then you have what will endure when the storms come. Then you will be able to swim to shore safely. If my husband, Greg, had not been rescued after his boating accident, the result could truly have been tragic. This may be a moment when you are being called on to rescue your family.

To achieve powerful life changes, we need to be willing to work together. I am so humbled and grateful that people who don't share my faith are reaching out by helping others with financial and health crises. Whether it is a program offered by a large foundation or something as small as sending a dollar for needle and thread that will aid babies in need, we can make a difference by combining our efforts and working with others. Be open to listening to people who are different. When I modeled, I often wondered why God placed me in that business. The fashion industry was not something I sought to be a part of. It seemed frivolous. My mom was a nurse, my dad worked in the labor industry, my husband saved lives as an emergency room physician. At the end of the day, my big achievement was to think of a new pose.

Then I realized that God might have put me where I was so that I would have the opportunity to examine and strengthen my values. Being around people who were different from me gave me a new perspective. It helped me open my arms and my heart to people who didn't necessarily see things the way I did. Our job as Christians is not to judge other people. The Lord says, "Do not judge, or you too will be judged" (Matthew 7:1). We're going to disagree on things. It's important that those disagreements be honored with civility and respect. If we can have an open dialogue about real problems and find real solutions without being hurtful to one another, we have a great opportunity to rebuild not only our financial wealth, but also our emotional and spiritual wealth.

I have a friend who has this special ability to speak and work with anyone. Nick Vujicic is an author, lecturer, motivational speaker, and pastor. He is also a man born without arms or legs. He travels around the world, inspiring people with his message of crossing boundaries, breaking down barriers, and bringing people to the love and hope found in Jesus. When you are with someone like Nick, who refuses to see any kind of limitation in his life, it's easier to understand that our financial crisis is not what we fear it to be. Nick's organization is called Life Without Limbs. To me, his is a life without limits.

I grew up hearing my father say that he was the richest man in the world. For a long time I was embarrassed and didn't want people to know that we were so rich. I finally realized that in fact we didn't have much money. What my father was saying was, "Thank You, Lord, for making me the richest man in the world because of the blessings of my family." My friend Nick is another of the richest people on this planet. It has nothing to do with material success, but his role as a ray of light for the Lord and his gift for turning what some people see as disability into powerful abilities and possibilities.

As you look at your bank balance and credit card statement and 401(k), think about the possibilities there for you. Look to people like Nick who are changing the world despite the obstacles in their lives. Remember that our troubles are always an opportunity to run into the open arms of our Lord. No matter how bleak your situation, He has the power to restore and lift you up: "Those who hope in the LORD will renew their strength. They will soar on wings like eagles" (Isaiah 40:31).

Whenever we travel by plane, a few members of our business family experience an emotional reaction to turbulence. I try to encourage them to remember that turbulence is part of the process. I believe with absolute certainty in God's ability to have us land safely. Though we may see our bodies tossed about, we don't have to let that turbulence rock our world. My heartfelt prayer for you is that whenever you encounter turbulence in your journey, the Lord's angels will wrap their loving wings around you, and you will experience a safe, smooth, and soft landing. God bless you.

Love,
kathy

notes

Chapter 1: Money Matters

1. Ben Woolsey, "Credit card industry facts and personal debt statistics 2006–07," CreditCards.com, http://www.credit cards.com/statistics/credit-card-industry-facts-and-personal-debt-statistics.php (accessed January 29, 2008).

2. Ibid.

Chapter 3: Your Healthy Home

1. Stephanie Nano, "Obese Kids May Face Heart Risks Later," ABC News, December 6, 2007, http://abcnews.go .com/Health/wireStory?id=3965957 (accessed May 23, 2008).

2. Adapted from "Menopause," Medicine Plus, U.S. National Library of Medicine and National Institutes of Health, http://www.nlm.nih.gov/medlineplus/ency/article/000894 .htm (accessed February 19, 2008).

Chapter 4: Safe at Home

1. "Trends in Unintentional Childhood Injury Deaths," Safe Kids USA, http://www.usa.safekids.org/tier3_cd_2c .cfm?content_item_id=19011&folder_id=540 (accessed January 29, 2008).

2. "Child Passenger Safety: Fact Sheet," Department of

Health and Human Services, Centers for Disease Control and Prevention, http://www.cdc.gov/ncipc/factsheets/childpas .htm (accessed January 29, 2008).

3. Vehicle, water, fire, and suffocation safety tips adapted from Safe Kids USA, http://www.usa.safekids.org/tier2_rl .cfm?folder_id=166 (accessed January 29, 2008).

4. Margery Williams, *The Velveteen Rabbit* (Philadelphia: Running Press, 1989), 22.

5. Associated Press, "Study: More kids exposed to online porn," MSNBC, February 5, 2007, http://www.msnbc.msn .com/id/16981028/ (accessed January 29, 2008).

6. Jeff Chu, "You Wanna Take This Online?" *Time*, August 8, 2005, 52–53.

7. Associated Press, "Mom: Girl killed herself over online hoax," MSNBC, November 19, 2007, http://www.msnbc .msn.com/id/21844203/ (accessed January 29, 2008).

8. "Sexual Health Statistics for Teenagers and Young Adults in the United States," Kaiser Family Foundation, September 2006, http://www.kff.org/womenshealth/upload/3040-03 .pdf (accessed January 29, 2008).

9. Safety tips on falls, poisonings, and firearms adapted from Safe Kids USA, http://www.usa.safekids.org/tier2_rl .cfm?folder_id=166 (accessed January 29, 2008).

10. Associated Press, "Millions of young abusing cough medicine," *USA Today*, January 9, 2008, http://www.usatoday .com/news/health/2008-01-09-cough-medicine-abuse_N.htm (accessed May 23, 2008).

11. Mary Frances Bowley, *A League of Dangerous Women* (Colorado Springs, CO: Multnomah, 2006), 141–153.

Chapter 5: Your Best You

1. Jone Johnson Lewis, "Lucille Ball Quotes," About.com, http://womenshistory.about.com/od/quotes/a/lucille_ball.htm (accessed May 23, 2008).

2. Isabel Wolseley, *Daily Guideposts 2002* (New York: Guideposts, 2002).

Chapter 6: No I in Mom

1. Kathy Peel, *Desperate Households* (Carol Stream, IL: Tyndale, 2007), 208–209.